Government in the Classroom: Dollars and Power in Education

Proceedings of
The Academy of
Political Science

Volume 33
Number 2

Edited by Mary Frase Williams

New York, 1978

Contents

Preface

This project had its inception in a newspaper account that quoted a Long Island school board member as saying that 80 percent of the budget of the local school district was mandated by the federal and state governments or by contracts with the teachers' union. The board had discretion in spending only 20 percent of the budget. While the accuracy of these percentages might be questioned, there can be no doubt that mandated programs determined the expenditure of the major part of public school budgets.

Not all school board members are unhappy with this situation. Undoubtedly the excuse that a particular program was mandated has been used to fend off pressures from constituents and to justify tax increases. Although a school board still had a fifth of the budget to spend as it chose, even the responsibility for these expenditures sometimes could be shifted to the federal or state governments or the teachers' union.

Persons concerned about the large portion of mandated school expenditures are often faced with the argument that local school boards have long been dominated by professional superintendents of schools and in fact rarely initiate new ideas or make independent decisions. In matters of professional concern, perhaps the lay board ought to be guided by the advice of the superintendent who, in theory at least, knows more about educational matters than it does. However, the board always had the power to dismiss the superintendent if it wished and to hire another more to its liking. Indeed, in any situation involving professionals and a lay board, whether in the area of health, the military, or fiscal professionals, somewhat the same relationship develops. The present situation faced by school boards is entirely different if the ultimate power of decision in most cases regarding spending is taken from the local board and placed in other hands. Further to complicate this situation is the fact that while the basic laws are passed by Congress, the detailed regulations interpreting and implementing the law are issued by a bureaucracy that is not responsible to the voters.

The National Education Association lobbied vigorously for federal aid, and at first many local educational administrators welcomed it. But they were dismayed to find that federal regulation followed the federal dollar. What this has meant at the local level is described in some detail in one of the essays in this volume by William C. French, a school superintendent. Moreover, government regulations are normally drafted by attorneys who are concerned about the protection of citizen rights and the possibility that the regulations may be challenged in the courts. Consequently, they are greatly concerned with defining the rights of parents and of children, outlining lines of appeal, and ensuring that the record be detailed and clear. One by-product, then, has been a tremendous amount of paperwork that on occasion may reduce the actual teaching services.

One obvious result of federal involvement in education has been a vast increase in the size of the government bureaucracy. In Washington, the moribund Office of Education launched a recruiting program that stripped personnel from the already weak state departments of education and established regional offices to monitor federal programs. Soon local school districts in search of federal money found it advisable to establish liaison staffs, not only in Washington but also in the regional offices, as well as in the state capitals. While the very size of the American public school system made compliance with federal regulations difficult, the detailed and sometimes conflicting federal directives also stimulated, and indeed made necessary, an increase in administrative staffs of local school districts.

As these essays indicate, there is good reason to believe that local school districts in many cases were successful in evading compliance, either through ignorance or obstinate resistance. In the last decade, for example, the national government spent $14 billion in research and development to improve teaching methods. Quite apart from the question of whether its efforts would indeed have improved methods, a study of six hundred school districts conducted by the Rand Corporation revealed little change in classroom procedures. One explanation might be that, while young teachers were interested in change, older ones, with whom decisions rested, were more inclined to continue teaching as they had in the past. To be sure, one must admit that a decade is a brief interval in the life of a federal program—perhaps much too brief to evaluate fully the success or failure of a new government program.

Other essays seem to indicate that some professional educators welcomed what they regard as trends to centralize control of education. They argue that few local school board members have the ability to make intelligent decisions in an area as important as education. Moreover, they point out that school boards are frequently chosen through elections in which a very small proportion of the registered voters participate. Thus the board is more likely to represent special interest groups than a broad-based cross section of the public. On the positive side, they argue that a highly centralized national system of education would remove the present inequities of financing local schools through the property tax. Some districts have a great deal of tax-producing property and few children, while others have a great many children and a small tax base. A national system would also integrate the schools on racial and economic lines, since districts could be extended across municipal boundaries. Readers who hold these views will find the essay describing the highly centralized system in

Israel especially provocative, since it raises doubts as to whether that course of action will bring about the improvements its advocates expect.

The most controversial federal program has been the one concerned with enlarging opportunities for physically or mentally handicapped children by placing them in the mainstream of the educational process. None would question the intent of the program, but a number of the essays emphasize the burdens that its detailed regulations have placed on the schools.

The impact of government programs on private schools has received little public attention. One essay calls attention to the impact of inflation on private school financing. Some government programs also affect private as well as public schools. One result has been to increase tuition charges. In the past, many parents of children in private schools have made gifts in their support that were exempt from taxation under the Internal Revenue Code. With increased tuition costs, parents no longer feel able to make these contributions, particularly since they have already paid income taxes on the tuition charges.

Throughout these essays there is an underlying tone of unhappiness with government in the classroom. Although the authors are professional educators who welcomed government dollars, they were distressed by the power that accompanied them. One essay argues that government control of education need not follow the government dollar. This is wishful thinking, as the experience of a hundred other government programs indicates.

Finally, well-intentioned efforts to solve some problems have led to new and unforeseen problems. Perhaps, as one author states, most of the present complaints will disappear as the bureaucracy gains experience. This is certainly a desirable goal toward which to work.

The authors of these essays are affiliated with various universities, research organizations, and government agencies. The views they express, however, are their own and do not necessarily reflect those of the institutions with which they are associated or those of the Academy.

The Academy wishes to express its appreciation to Professor Mary Frase Williams, who organized the project and edited the essays, and to William Farr, Frederick Wegener, and Arthur Adler for their editorial assistance. The Academy is also indebted to Dr. Frank Macchiarola, chancellor of the New York City schools, who chaired the sessions of the conference held at Columbia University on this topic. A distinguished group of persons participated in the conference panels. Among them were Nancy Jacobs, president of the Board of Education, Demarest, New Jersey; Gerald Benjamin, associate professor of political science, State University College at New Paltz; Susan Fuhrman, adjunct assistant professor of politics and education, Teachers College, Columbia University; John B. Poster, associate professor of urban education, Fordham University; and Dale Mann, professor and chairperson of educational administration, Teachers College, Columbia University.

ROBERT H. CONNERY
President of the Academy

Contributors

JOEL S. BERKE is Senior Research Scientist, Education Policy Research Institute of the Educational Testing Service, and former Deputy Assistant Secretary, Department of Health, Education, and Welfare for Education Policy Development.

DONALD W. BURNES is Team Leader for Legal and Governmental Studies in the program on Educational Policy and Organization sponsored by the National Institute of Education.

ROBERT H. CONNERY is Professor Emeritus of Public Law and Government, Columbia University, and President, the Academy of Political Science.

ELIZABETH J. DEMAREST is Policy Analyst, staff of the Assistant Secretary for Education, Department of Health, Education, and Welfare.

BRUCE DOLLAR is Research Associate for the Center for Policy Research, Inc., in New York City.

BARBARA DWYER is Research Associate, Education Turnkey Systems, Inc., in Washington, D.C. She has participated in several policy research studies dealing with the education of the handicapped.

WILLIAM C. FRENCH is Superintendent of Schools, New Canaan, Connecticut.

JAMES W. GUTHRIE is Professor of Education, University of California at Berkeley.

MICHAEL W. KIRST is Associate Professor of Education and Business Administration, Stanford University. He is also President of the California State Board of Education.

FREDERICK S. LANE is Assistant Professor of Public Administration and Political Science and Director of Institutional Research, Baruch College, City University of New York.

LORRAINE M. McDONNELL, who is on the staff of the Rand Corporation, has worked on several studies of state-level implementation of federal educational programs.

ANTHONY H. PASCAL, formerly the head of the Office of Economic Research, U.S. Department of Commerce, is Director of Human Resource Studies, the Rand Corporation.

ELAD PELED, formerly Director-General, Ministry of Education and Culture, Israel, is Senior Lecturer, Department of Education, Ben Gurion University. He is editor of *Education in Israel in the 1980's.*

BERYL A. RADIN is Associate Professor, Washington Public Affairs Center, University of Southern California. She is the author of *Implementation, Change and the Federal Bureaucracy: School Desegregation Policy in HEW, 1964-68.*

JOEL D. SHERMAN is Research Director, School Finance Project, Lawyers' Committee for Civil Rights Under Law. He has served as a consultant to the Organization for Economic Cooperation and Development.

JANET M. SIMONS is Research Associate, Education Turnkey Systems, Inc., in Washington, D.C. She has participated in several policy research studies dealing with the education of the handicapped.

HARVEY J. TUCKER, Assistant Professor of Political Science at Texas A&M University, is coauthor of *The Quest for Responsive Government.*

THOMAS VITULLO-MARTIN is a consultant to the National Institute of Education and to the Ford Foundation. He is the author of the forthcoming book *Inner City Private Schools: Financing and Governance.*

MARY FRASE WILLIAMS, a member of the faculty of Teachers College, Columbia University, in the Politics and Education Program, is a consultant to the National Conference of State Legislatures.

L. HARMON ZEIGLER is Professor of Political Science, the University of Oregon, and a program director at the Center for Educational Policy and Management. He is coauthor of *Governing American Schools.*

American Education and Federalism

MARY FRASE WILLIAMS

Education has always been highly valued by Americans, both as an end in itself and as a means to other ends, such as mobility, equality, and Americanization. This faith in education may account in part for the early establishment in the United States of public support for the schools. Historically, the educational system has been a decentralized one, with control and financing centered in the local school district, administered by a locally elected school board. Local control of education is deeply ingrained in American tradition.

The system of governance, however, is a federal one, with the involvement of all three levels of government in education. Questions about the relationships among the levels of government have become increasingly important as first the state and then the federal roles in education have grown and the governance of education has become more and more centralized. The extent to which control has shifted away from the local level can be seen in the role of the courts in issues such as integration and school finance, the role of the federal government in special education, the conditions attached to acceptance of federal aid, and the role of the state in areas such as licensing of teachers and curriculum requirements. At the same time that some activists were demanding decentralization of large-city school districts in the name of greater local control, other observers were beginning to question the vitality and relevance of local school boards.

Many people have decried these developments, but systematic and comprehensive treatments of the issues have been lacking. The available materials tend to be subjective, to represent a particular point of view and to serve a political purpose, or, if scholarly, to deal with limited aspects of the problem. This volume provides an overview of the current state of the governance of education with an emphasis on the intergovernmental dimensions of educational policy and governance. The authors and topics were chosen so as to provide a diversity of viewpoints, perspectives, and backgrounds, as well as a comprehensive picture of the current and future state of educational governance.

The authors have not restricted themselves simply to describing and analyzing certain issues, but many have also presented their recommendations for future courses of action. Given the variety of perspectives of the authors—including a local school superintendent, the chairman of a state board of education, federal officials, university professors, and private researchers and consultants—it is not surprising that their conclusions and recommendations are also diverse and sometimes contradictory.

For many years it was alleged that education was and should be above the corrupting influences of politics. While this notion was a powerful one in its heyday and was perpetuated by educators, at least in part because it served their own interest, both scholars and the public have come to realize in recent years that the educational system is highly political. The issues of governance, control, and intergovernmental relations assessed in these essays constitute the essence of politics; they involve questions of power, or, in Lasswell's terms, Who gets what, when, and how?

Education in America

Education has occupied a unique position among public services in the United States, particularly with respect to its governance. Perhaps far more than any other function, "local control" has been the hallmark of American public education. Furthermore, there is an emphasis on lay control, as opposed to political or professional control, which is not found in other functions. In terms of governance, schools are typically set apart from the rest of local government, and educational structures differ from those of other functions. Finally, and perhaps related to the others, is the enormous faith in and value placed on education by the American culture.

This primacy of education can be seen in a variety of ways. One indicator is the establishment of schools and other institutions intended to provide educational instruction from the very beginning of the colonies; government involvement in education followed very shortly. Government support and regulation of education predated a similar role in most of the other services now provided by one level of government or another in the United States. Another indication of the importance and prominence of education is the magnitude of the education enterprise relative to the entire economy or to the public sector. Local governments spend far more on education than on any other function, and, in fact, except in the largest cities, public schools typically account for more than half the local budget. At the state level, education absorbs more of the state budget than any other function.

Other indicators of the commitment to education are that educational expenditures (both public and private) for all levels, including higher education, now hover between 7 and 8 percent of the GNP (double the rate of twenty-five years ago), and spending for public elementary and secondary education constitutes over 5 percent of personal income. Furthermore, among employee organizations, the National Education Association's membership is second only to the

Teamsters'. Despite the school consolidation movement, there are still over sixteen thousand school districts in the nation (1975–76), and until the 1972 Census of Governments, school districts were the most numerous type of governmental unit in this country.

From the days of the early colonies until the 1960s, Americans looked to education as the means of solving their most pressing national problems or achieving their most cherished goals. For the Puritans, education was an instrument of religion. In the early days of the Republic, education was seen as the means of achieving political goals, developing the enlightened citizenry necessary for a democracy, and assimilating the increasing number of immigrants. In the late nineteenth century, economic growth was added to the contributions that schools were expected to make. Through much of the nation's history, education has been seen as a means of socioeconomic mobility and a way to equalize the opportunities for Americans from all backgrounds. Finally, in the second half of the twentieth century, education has been expected to overcome the handicaps of discrimination and poverty.

However, many now question the wisdom of educators and the efficacy of education. A number of factors appear to have contributed to this change in mood: declining test scores, escalating costs, conflicts in education over what are seen as social rather than educational problems such as desegregation, prayer in schools, the increasing militancy of teachers and the incidence of teacher strikes, a general decline of trust in government and public officials, the apparent failure of the social programs of the 1960s, and perhaps the major issue of concern in this volume, a feeling of loss of local control over public schools. The declining birthrate and aging population have resulted in a decreasing segment of the population directly concerned with public education. One apparent by-product of these developments is a declining rate of approval by the voters of school budgets, taxes, and bonds. Another indicator is legislative and public support for limitations on spending and taxation, either for education specifically or government in general.

Education is unique among local public services with respect to its structure of governance. While most services are administered as part of the local general unit of government—town, county, village, township, or city—education is an exception. The typical pattern is the existence of an independent school district, separate from all other units of government, with the power to levy taxes for the support of elementary and secondary schools. Responsibility for governing this entity lies with an elected lay board of education. While other functions may occasionally be governed by a separate board or may operate out of a separate unit of government, education is the only one that is consistently divorced from the general purpose unit of local government in this way:

The public also has a greater and more direct role in the governance of education than in any other service. Not only are school board members elected, but school taxes and bond issues are also voted on in many places. However, lay control over education is considerably less than it was in the early days of the Republic, when there were no professional administrators. The increasing size and complexity of education led first to the development of principals and then superintendents to run schools and school districts.

It must be remembered, however, that local school districts do not have a life of their own apart from the dictates of the state. School districts are created to serve the state in fulfilling its responsibility for public education. They derive their authority from the state, and their existence, structure, power, organization, and even boundaries are subject to state dictates and regulation. While states have delegated much of the management and operation of the schools to local school districts, they can reclaim or change those powers if and when they choose. Thus, school districts are creatures of the state, and school board members are state agents, although they have a dual role, serving their local constituents as well.

History of American Public Education

While education in the earliest days of the colonies was largely a private endeavor, the responsibility of the family and the church, public provision and support of education also began very early, especially in Massachusetts and the rest of New England. Similarly, while education was primarily a local effort for the first two centuries, the evolution toward a federal system also began early with some involvement of first the state and then the national government in education. In 1635 the Boston Latin School was founded and was partially financed by town funds. The following year the General Court, the colonial legislature, contributed funds to the institution that was to become Harvard University. In 1642 and 1647 the General Court required first the provision of education by parents and masters and then the establishment of schools, but attendance in the schools was not compulsory. The 1647 act mandated that all towns of at least fifty families appoint a teacher of reading and writing and that all with more than one hundred families also establish a secondary school. These schools were to be supported by the masters, parents, or the inhabitants in general. Thus the principle of local taxation for the financing of schools was also established quickly. In general, however, public funds provided only part of the revenues, and the rest came from tuition, fees, and private benevolence. The other New England colonies followed the lead of Massachusetts, but in the rest of the colonies (and continuing in the first years of the new nation), public provision of education was limited to orphans and the poor. Other children, if they did not come from well-to-do families, received their education at home or through apprenticeships, while children of the rich were tutored, attended private schools, or were sent abroad for their education.

The measures enacted by the Massachusetts General Court represented the first state-level involvement in public education. However, the nature of that involvement was to require actions by local governments, without any state financial contribution to the schools.

The first federal level initiative in the field of public education came under the Articles of Confederation and did involve financial support for education. The Land Ordinance of 1785 specified that one section out of every township in the Northwest Territory be set aside for education. Later states received two or four sections with other lands for this purpose. The sale and rental of these lands were to support education, and the revenues went to the state. The federal Constitution did not mention education, although in later years federal activities in this field have been justified under the broad phrase "provide for the common Defence and the general Welfare."

The Tenth Amendment reserved to the states powers not explicitly granted to the federal government, including the responsibility for education. However, the states did not assume an active role until much later, and again the initial leadership was provided by the New England states. Massachusetts established a state board of education in 1837, and Horace Mann was appointed the secretary of the board. Along with other reformers, Mann and Henry Barnard, who occupied a similar position in Connecticut, waged the battle for the establishment of common schools—elementary schools that would be free, publicly supported, and open to all children—and for a more vigorous state presence in education. Gradually an increasing number of states included in their constitutions language related to the provision of public education. Particularly in the northern states, the middle part of the nineteenth century saw both the fruition of the common school movement and the centralization of control at the state level in the hands of state boards and superintendents of schools. Free universal public schools did not become a reality in the South, however, until after the Civil War.

In the last third of the nineteenth century the extension of public education took the form of secondary schools and attendance laws. The addition of public high schools and the gradual enactment of compulsory attendance laws meant considerable growth in school attendance in the late 1800s. These developments continued into the twentieth century until free public education through high school and required attendance through the early high school years became universal.

In 1862 Congress passed the Morrill Act, which gave each state public lands to be used to support higher education in the areas of "agriculture and the mechanic arts" and was the basis for the establishment of the land-grant colleges. It also presaged the nature of future federal aid to education. Federal dollars would be targeted for specific uses, rather than leaving the discretion as to how to spend the money to the recipients of the funds at the state or local level. Other major examples of categorical aid, as opposed to general aid, were the Smith-Hughes Act of 1917, providing federal funds for vocational education, and the National Defense Education Act of 1958, which was primarily concerned with instruction in mathematics, science, and foreign languages. The federal program closest to being general aid is impact aid, initiated during World War II, which provides federal grants to districts with large numbers of federal employees or installations. Impact aid provides both aid for construction and operating expenses.

The U. S. Office of Education (OE) was established in 1867, but it was largely an information-gathering agency that had little impact on local school districts until the passage of the Elementary and Secondary Education Act of 1965 (ESEA). Federal aid to education rose dramatically with ESEA, and OE had to change and expand in order to assume the new and much larger role resulting from ESEA.

Centralization and Local Control

The early 1800s marked the era of greatest decentralization and diversity in American education. There was enormous variation within the original colonies in the provision, content, and goals of education, reflecting the diverse backgrounds of the settlers of the different colonies. This variation continued in the early days of the Republic. The first schools had been locally founded and controlled, and the local units became smaller and more independent as settlers moved away from the seacoast. For example, schools were initially established in New England under the auspices of the towns, but as migration away from the original centers of population occurred, the town schools became too distant for children in the new settlements. Schools were established in the outlying "districts," and the eventual result was the legal recognition of school districts as independent of the towns and empowered to raise taxes to support the schools. General town officials were originally responsible for governing education in the New England colonies, but distinct governing bodies gradually evolved as the result of both the separation of school districts from towns and the increasing demands of the task. These New England school committees were the forerunners of the present-day school board.

Most of the developments in education since the early 1800s have lessened decentralization, both within and across states. The common school movement contributed to a greater standardization in the access to and content of public elementary education. The greater role of the state, both in providing financial assistance and setting standards, reduced the discretion of local school officials about the kind of education they would provide. The movement to consolidate small school districts, often required by the state or at least encouraged by state financial incentives, also reduced the decentralization of American education. Increasing professionalization in education has also had a strong centralizing effect, as national and professional standards and expectations have replaced local or regional ones. The expansion of the federal role in education in the last twenty years, as described in several of the essays in this collection, has been the latest development contributing to a more centralized system of educational governance.

Financing as well as the management of education has also become more centralized. The local share in financing public schools has declined during the twentieth century. The state contribution has risen gradually in the last seventy-five years, and the federal share rose significantly in 1965 when ESEA was passed. Since it is categorical aid, federal aid is generally more restrictive in the way it may be used than is state aid. The states give local school districts both general and categorical aid, but the bulk is general aid, and the utilization of state categorical monies is often poorly monitored. Despite the unmistakable centralizing trend, however, it is important to remember that the United States educational system remains among the most decentralized in the world.

As the previous discussion has indicated, several of the distinctive aspects of education are currently being challenged or are undergoing change. This is particularly true with regard to local control and the privileged status of education. Is local control of education now more a myth than a reality? How extensively has local control of education changed in the 1960s and 1970s? These questions cannot be ignored, because they represent the most fundamental issues in educational governance today.

This collection of essays explores a variety of issues related to the governmental role in education, especially the apparent decline in local control. What has been gained and lost by centralization? What are the problems related to government regulation and intergovernmental relations with regard to specific educational issues such as integration, school finance, and special education? Has the growth in the strength of teacher organizations reduced the discretion of local school officials? The first section of this volume deals with the diminution of the local role in education and the nature of state and federal roles. The second section examines the role of government in a variety of specific issue areas. Finally, the third section describes the experience of Israel's highly centralized educational system.

Local Control Under Attack

WILLIAM C. FRENCH

In 1642 colonial officials in Massachusetts required town officials to see that children were taught "learning and labor" and in 1647 required every town of fifty freeholders to appoint a teacher in reading and writing. It is quite possible that no later than 1648 town officials were complaining about "outside" interference in the operation of the local schools.

Free public education is now a major national undertaking, and three hundred years of experience have worked to define more clearly a means of providing a national public school system controlled by a unique balance of power among the local communities, the states, and the federal government. As a result, current arguments about who should control public education generally do not consider the complete exclusion of any level of government. However, the matter of the relative roles of all levels remains a vital issue, and at this point in history there is reason to be deeply concerned about recent trends that strongly indicate a major shift in this balance.

Historically, American states and communities have successfully resisted direct federal control of the public schools. The Constitution leaves education to the states by design. Within the states, a balance between community control and state control has evolved; and while states vary, in nearly all cases a considerable degree of authority over educational programs has been delegated to the local community and its representatives on boards of education. In return, local boards of education have generally been responsive to the role of the federal government, and the right of the state government, to define the needs of the nation and the state and work with local school systems to develop educational programs related to these broad public needs.

On the other hand, local boards of education are in need of state and federal financial assistance. Few, if any, local communities and boards can rely totally on the local tax structure as the only means of support for the local educational program. Thus the combination of relatively broad program direction from state and federal governments and financial assistance from or through the states has been the basis for an effective partnership between local communities and higher levels of government. Critical to this partnership has been the latitude allowed local school systems in educational programs.

The Balance of Control

In recent years, two forces have emerged that threaten the balance among the various levels of government with regard to the control of education. The first of these relates to the increasing efforts of the federal government to resolve broad societal problems in ways that utilize the public schools as the vehicle for action. There is no question about the right and responsibility of the federal and state governments to confront the problems of the poor, minorities, women, the physically handicapped, and the emotionally and educationally deprived, as well as other equally important social and civil concerns. However, those interested in maintaining local control of school programs are increasingly concerned about whether the public schools are always the appropriate vehicle through which to confront all these issues and the mounting impact of the governmentally mandated programs on the direction of local school systems.

One does not need to understand totally the intricacies of the various federal laws to recognize that legislative efforts to deal with these important concerns have a significant impact on the direction of educational programs. It is this latter point that is particularly difficult for local school systems. States that accept federally supported programs must also accept specific requirements for the operation of these programs, and the impact reaches directly into local program offerings. Often a negative effect results because:

• Funding for mandated programs is usually insufficient to permit the local school system to do a good job. As a result, local systems have to commit already scarce local funds to these programs at the expense of the rest of the curricular offering.

• Mandated programs are often designed to deal with the needs of a special group of pupils that differ from the needs of the majority of students.

• Mandated programs tend to be standardized, inflexible, and legalistically designed.

• An almost fanatic concern for accountability results in a blizzard of the most complex reporting forms imaginable.

To illustrate the effect of increased federal involvement on local school programs, one needs to examine what can happen to an actual school system under the provisions of a federally designed program. The example that follows represents the experiences of one Connecticut school system after the implementation of PL 94–142.

PL 94–142, an extension of the Rehabilitation Act of 1973, is directed toward providing educational programs for the handicapped. In Connecticut, PL 94–142 supplements previously existing state funded programs for physically, emotionally, or socially handicapped children in need of special education. The funds from the federal government are allocated to the individual states, and through the state to each individual school system on the basis of a predesigned local plan for utilizing these funds.

During the 1977–78 school year the local school system cited here as an example received $17,000 under the provisions of PL 94–142. With this funding, the school system was able to provide a number of new or expanded services. These included additional psychological and social services, an alternative evening high school, and added opportunities for the placement of pupils in severe need in special schools. In general, the "flow-through" funds provided from federal and state sources did make some valuable additional programs and services possible.

However, this gift was not without cost to the local school system. For example, along with the special funding has come a much more complex system of record-keeping, the establishment of more rigid procedures, and an elaborate set of specific requirements. As for the impact on people, adaption to the federal requirements resulted in a marked increase in frustration on the part of both parents and professional personnel. It is this latter point that dramatizes one major problem related to specific program mandates.

Prior to the passage of PL 94–142, this school system successfully placed a high priority on close and informal relationships between the schools and the parents. This relationship was particularly important in dealing with the sensitive issues surrounding those students who need special education services. To maintain this relationship the staff members tried to establish an environment for school-parent conferences that was nonlegalistic and nonthreatening. While parents have always had the right to appeal recommendations of the planning and placement team meetings to the board of of education, and ultimately to the State Department of Education, the processes by which agreement on programs was reached were managed in a way that minimized the adversary relationship between parents and the school. The success of this process rested largely on the judgment and the skill of the professional people involved and their sensitivity to the problems that parents and students faced in acquiring an education. What the system lacked in form and format it made up for in genuine relationships between the school personnel and the parents and children being served.

Perhaps the major cost to the school system in adapting to the regulations of PL 94–142 has been the diminishment of this close relationship between the school and parents of children who need special educational programs. It is not unusual now to deal more directly with attorneys than with parents. There is an increasing concern about form and procedure. Adversary relationships are practically ensured as a result of due-process procedures that encourage parents to "challenge" and to increase the emphasis on "defense" on the part of school people.

The school system has encouraged good faith in negotiations regarding a child's evaluation, identification, and placement as a matter of long-standing principle, but in recent months resistance and suspicion have increased. Parents often resort to the use of due-process regulations to force a conclusion that may not always be in the best interest of the child.

A second difficulty resulting from the implementation of PL 94–142 relates to the amount and quality of services offered. The ritualistic and legalistic effects of this act have resulted in a significant increase in the amount of professional time devoted to "planning and placement" meetings. There has been a 25 to 50 percent increase in the number of such meetings with the net result that, among the sixteen special education-trained staff members, well over two thousand hours of professional time per year are withdrawn from direct services to children.

The main point of this review is to note that while it is extremely important to protect the rights of students and parents in the process of providing education for children with learning disabilities, the new federal and state requirements are excessively restrictive and overly structured. The net result is a significant loss in the quality of the program provided the students. The major contribution of federal involvement has been to add to the form and formality of the process at the expense of the delivery of services to special education children.

It should be noted that other (nonspecial education) children are being affected by this change. The services of the special education professional staff had been available to a considerable degree to children within the mainstream of the educational program. With the increasing expectations set upon the local school system PL 94–142, it is clear that the bulk of the time available from the special education staff is now concentrated on students formally identified as having special education needs. Little time is available for students in the mainstream of the education program who may also have need for these services but who are not formally considered "special education" pupils.

A second series of events affecting the relative position of the various levels of government involved in the management of schools concerns the decisions by state supreme courts in regard to the provision of equal educational opportunities within the various states. Historically, public education has been financed to a significant degree by local property taxes. While local taxes have been supplemented by state aid in varying degrees in the different states, differences in property wealth among communities have been considered a major factor in determining the difference in the quality of the educational program and services. In several states, courts have held that heavy reliance on the local property tax has created inequitable educational opportunities in direct conflict with state constitutional guarantees.

As a result, state legislatures have been directed to find a means to finance public education that would more nearly equalize opportunities for all students. The first responses to these court decisions in terms of legislative actions have been to seek sources of funding other than the local property tax. In this process, some states have also sought ways to restrict or limit previously economically favored communities. For example, ceilings, generally termed "caps," have been placed on expenditures or tax rates, and existing state aid has been reduced or withdrawn. Needless to say, the communities concerned have reacted strongly to this treatment since (a) they believe differences in overall expenditures between communities largely results from a difference in the general costs of goods and services between different areas of a state, (b) they argue districts should have the right to spend more on education and strive for greater excellence if they wish, and (c) they have been forced to reduce local programs significantly. Clearly, the reduction of local school program offerings is regarded as a significant intrusion of state regulation into local school affairs.

Even more disturbing has been the tendency in some states for legislators and the state department of education to combine added or revised systems of funding with increased centralization of control of educational programs. For example, the state of Connecticut is experiencing strong reactions to proposals developed by the State Department of Education that appear to link a recent court decision on school finance with educational programs in a manner that significantly increases the role of the state department in the determination of all programs. The state department's introductory review describes the proposals in this manner: "Strengthening the local-state partnership in public education in Connecticut, to provide for each child the 'suitable program of educational experiences' required by law, is the persistent theme of 26 recommendations developed by the Education Department's Task Force on Educational Equity."[1] Included in the report are recommendations that propose state involvement in matters ranging through essentially every aspect of local school operation.

Although still in proposal form, there is little doubt in the minds of many across the state that these recommendations represent an effort to change significantly the relationship between the State Education Department and the local schools. Typical of this point of view is the reaction of the executive director of the Connecticut Association of Boards of Education:

> The draft report reveals a distrust of local communities, a fear that those communities, which will still raise more than 50 percent of all funds to run the local schools, will spend money unwisely, wastefully, and not in the best interests of the children. The Task Force has recommended an approach that will lead to standardization, not excellence, in our schools, and an expensive state bureaucracy maintained not so much to assist local communities, but to monitor them. As the commissioner stated, Connecticut's school districts are among the best in the country. The State Department proposes sweeping changes in a system of governance that has been proven to be successful without any evidence that such change is needed or will result in the improvement of the education available to Connecticut's children.[2]

The Importance of the Community Role

In the light of what appear to be rapid shifts in the relative roles of the federal and state governments in regard to control of public education, there is a need to reinforce the importance of the part played by the local community and its board of education. If present trends continue, the nation may be in danger of losing a uniquely American democratic institution while settling for mediocrity in public education.

---

[1] Connecticut State Department of Education, *Issues and Answers*, vol. 2, no. 13, April 1978.

[2] Thomas Shannon, "A Power Grab Threatens Local Control," *American School Board Journal* (July 1978), p. 42.

Unfortunately, it is difficult to maintain a clear view about the relative merits of locally managed public schools. More than any other public institution, public education is surrounded by a large number of industries, foundations, research services, testing companies, and private consulting firms that subsist on the public schools. The very livelihood of these agencies often depends on finding "problems" and "weaknesses" in the school system. Thus the press is filled with critical reports about public education designed to justify the existence of these special interest groups.

Equally difficult to combat are the vested interests of governmental agencies— the state departments of education and, increasingly, the federal governmental departments. Large bureaucracies generally need to justify their existence. In the field of education this justification often involves probing for weaknesses and proposing remedies with considerable public fanfare. Again, the efforts of these agencies often result in negative conclusions about the accomplishments of locally controlled school systems.

Within this negative climate many individuals, organizations, and agencies have encouraged the view that locally controlled education is an antique that has outlived its purpose. Those who hold this view may well be wrong. It is distinctly possible that the present format for making educational decisions is, in fact, better than any other for dealing with present and future concerns about public institutions generally—and particularly the public schools. Increasingly, members of the public are expressing resentment about the intrusion of "big and distant government" into their lives and are expressing a strong desire to have a more direct voice in what public services should be and how they should be financed. The rising support for actions like Proposition 13 represents as much an emotional response to the loss of a direct say on the part of the public, as it does a revolt against rising personal property taxes. It is distinctly possible that the present structure of local boards of education is not only best suited to this climate but also may well serve as a model for other public services.

Critics of the current local structure for managing public education only look for its weaknesses, citing the wide variety of tough, controversial, and frustrating problems that surface at the local level as evidence that local boards of education are not capable of dealing with today's complex problems. When the public is allowed to select local citizens to make policy, confront issues in stormy public meetings, and make decisions within the turbulence of local community pressures, then issues are going to surface in a disturbing way. However, it is quite possible that many of these "problems" are the real issues facing the nation. Having a mechanism for dealing with them at the community level is critical to the health of a democratic society.

Those who feel that public education is too important to be left to citizen boards of education overlook the magnificent service this form of management has provided the country since the very beginning. There is the distinct possibility that the nation could be making a serious mistake in encouraging (or passively permitting) centralization of control. Locally controlled public education has significant strengths that, though often taken for granted, cannot be ignored. For example:

1. *The present local format for governing schools is as close to the public served as a governmental unit can come.* The opportunity for direct citizen involvement in the determination of public policy appears to be an increasingly important consideration for the present and future development of public institutions. Locally elected boards of education have been, and can continue to be, effective policy units.

Critics may contend that too often school boards are not the actual policymakers and that school superintendents have arrogated the real authority. Those who hold this view could benefit from the experience of holding the position. Whatever the appearances may be, few successful superintendents have any doubts about where the real authority lies. The record is quite definite and clear. A superintendent who does not satisfy his board most of the time will not hold the position for very long. The ultimate power of the local board, supported by tradition and law, is demonstrated to superintendents with disturbing frequency.

Members of local boards of education are among the unsung heroes of this country. They are citizens who volunteer their services because they care. When one considers the thousands of individuals across the land who are serving communities in this role, and the job they are asked to do, boards of education certainly have to be viewed as uniquely American democratic units of government.

2. *The present format is most responsive to differing public expectations about the educational program.* One of the greatest strengths of the locally oriented format is the flexibility it provides for adapting the educational program to community or regional expectations. In education, sameness is not necessarily goodness. There are real differences in the needs of different regions of the country, varying needs in different areas of a state, and disparate public expectations within communities. This diversity is an important fact of life in this country, and if public schools are to remain vital institutions, the ability to respond to local public priorities should be strengthened. The best education involves a solid melding of school and community goals. Schools should be an integral part of a community. If community needs relate to agriculture, then the school program should reflect this need. If community expectations lean heavily toward professions that require higher education in academic institutions, then the local school system should respond accordingly.

Experience indicates that the more distant the control of a program is from the local level, the greater the chance that the program will not meet the special needs of pupils. The classic example of this kind of situation can be found in the state and federally supported vocational programs. These programs were originally designed as an alternative to the classical academic high school program. However, over the years, federal and state control of these programs has resulted in a combination of arbitrary restrictions and curricular expectations that have created a rigid and independent adjunct to the local school program. Many pupils who might benefit the most from some kind of alternative secondary program are denied this opportunity. Local school systems have not been able to modify this situation and have had to develop other kinds of alternative programs locally to meet the real need of the youth of the community.

3. *Locally controlled education is more responsive to taxpayers.* In addition to being most responsive to citizens concerned about educational programs, the present locally controlled public school format is most responsive to those primarily concerned with costs and taxes. The American public continues to demand an active role in the determination of how much it is willing to pay for public services. The greater the distance between the taxpaying public and those who make decisions about how much and where tax money is spent, the greater the conflict on this issue becomes. As far as public education is concerned, the more that decisions about finance are removed to the state and federal level, the more likely there is to be a know-nothing type of public reaction against increased costs.

While current efforts to equalize educational opportunity must be approached on a statewide basis and will involve some shift in sources of funding away from local property taxes, it is unrealistic to assume that local funding will be totally eliminated as a source of support for public schools. Whatever emerges as the new pattern for school finance, some means must still be provided for citizen decisions regarding expenditures at the local level. The present local governmental structure, which generally provides for direct election of members of a board of education, annual public approval of the school budget, and an appeal process through a local referendum, is best designed to serve the needs and rights of the public in this area of concern.

4. *Locally controlled education is more responsive to human needs.* Perhaps the strongest argument for strengthening local control of education is the importance of the interrelationship between members of the community and the school. The heart of a successful school program rests to a considerable degree on the willingness and ability of the school to provide an appropriate educational program for the individual student. Critical to meeting this expectation is a close relationship between school personnel and parents. Any organizational form that contributes to this relationship is also contributing to the overall strength of the schools within a school system. Parents and citizens need to know that they have a stake in the school as parents and a responsibility for the school as taxpayers. Teachers, administrators, and board members need to feel responsible to the members of the community as clients and as citizens directly involved in financing the schools.

The thousands of school board members and school employees who live and work in small towns or small cities across the country know that, although it may sometimes be inconvenient and unreasonable, it is important for parents to share their problems and complaints and receive some responsible answers. It is true that the larger the community, the less effective this process may be, but even some of the largest cities have decentralized in an effort to recapture a part of this relationship. In any case, it is a relationship and a level of communication that must not be lost if schools are to be more than faceless institutions. Further loss of local control and responsibility would seriously weaken or destroy this intangible but valuable aspect of locally managed schools. The greater the opportunities for establishing conditions that encourage people to treat one another directly and humanely, the better the school program will be and the better the service to people will be. On the other hand, the more the power for decision-making about program and finance is shifted from the local communities to state and federal departments, the greater the indifference to individual concerns will be.

5. *Local control of school systems encourages excellence.* To date, experience with increasing intervention of state and federal agencies clearly indicates that any action by these agencies that combines financial aid with strict program requirements will, at best, only guarantee a quality of program no better than the average range of programs already provided within the state. On the other hand, in states or regions where schools have good support (including funding) and a high degree of local control, excellent programs have often emerged. While the so-called lighthouse school systems are generally located in economically favored areas, it is important to note that funding alone does not ensure excellence. Equally important is the ability of the community and school authorities to work together to identify needs and to develop good programs to meet those needs. One could argue that this latter element exists in most communities and if increased federal and state sources provide added assistance in funding to economically less favored communities without too many specific program controls, good programs relevant to local community needs will emerge. It can also be argued that increased regulation of local programs will never provide the opportunity for excellence, will diminish the relevance of programs in relation to local needs, and will discourage close school-community cooperation that is an essential element in the development and implementation of above average education programs.

Conclusion

This brief essay has presented the case for the retention of local control of public education programs. It maintains that the United States may already have gone too far in eroding local options. In fact, the nation may be in danger of losing a uniquely American democratic institution while settling for mediocrity in educational programs. An interesting parallel to contemplate relates to another unique institution. From colonial times, the town meeting has been a part of the governmental process for most New England towns. In recent years, however, some communities felt that this form of government had outlived its usefulness, since local citizens were not participating. As a result, a more complicated representative council form of government was substituted. Unfortunately, this change occurred just before or during a period of resurgence in citizen interest in being "involved"—an interest for which the town meeting was an ideal political vehicle. The net result of these changes has been the loss of a political system that was well suited for the current political climate at the local level. In the case of the governance of public education, the locally elected board of education is a national institution and, like the town meeting, is still the best format for dealing with the current level of interest and concern about the public schools.

The salvation of locally controlled public schools will require a reversal of current trends. It will require recognition by the American public of the value of this form of political organization and a conscious effort on the part of federal and state governments to preserve and strengthen this local institution.

At the federal level, Congress and the federal agencies need to reexamine what is happening to the federal-state relationship. Increasingly, federal legislation and the implementation of legislation are eroding the historic relationship between the federal government and the states. The federal government, with its enormous size, has power, momentum, and funding. Yet all concerned need to exercise restraint in the use of this power, if the proper balance is to be maintained between the federal government and the various states.

State governments have, by purposeful constitutional omission, the full responsibility for public education and full authority to direct this enterprise. States vary in the exercise of this power, but in general the preservation of local control of education depends on the willingness of state legislatures, state supreme courts, and state departments of education to act in a manner that strengthens the opportunity for local education program options. In more specific terms, while the federal and state governments have the responsibility and the right to attempt to define needs that are in the best interests of the nation and to expect public institutions—including the public schools—to examine programs in relation to those needs, both levels of government need to recognize that the best hope for success lies in permitting local school systems flexibility and latitude. In short, higher levels of government would be better advised to lay out the road map but leave the driving to the local school boards.

The question may be a matter of trust with regard to the ability and intentions of those responsible at the local level. If that is true, then state and federal legislators and administrative officials might find it instructive to spend some time on the line with school board members. They would generally find a large group of hard working citizen volunteers doing a tough job on behalf of their district, making decisions that combine the interests of the nation, the state, and the community in a manner that works as well as any democratic human endeavor.

The Myth of Lay Control

HARVEY J. TUCKER
L. HARMON ZEIGLER

The concept of a system of public schooling that is responsive to the citizenry and controlled by a democratically selected governing board is pervasive in the United States. This concept is reflected in the control of primary and secondary education by local governments, that is, school districts. Because of their unique position in the American federal system, their size, and their proximity to constituents, local governments are expected to be the most responsive. Thus, when the central queries of political science—who gets what, when, and how—are asked of school governance, one might expect that the distribution of influence would favor the lay public.

Most school districts are independent units of government, and their structures appear to offer the best possible conditions for citizen control. State education agencies are generally weak and capable of providing only limited leadership to the large number of local units they nominally oversee. The federal role in educational affairs is growing, but most important routine and episodic decisions are still made at the local level. Moreover, school districts can determine for themselves the quantity and quality of their educational services by exercising authority over taxing and expenditure levels, curriculum content, and personnel selection. In short, school districts have the autonomy necessary to respond to local preferences.

The opportunities for citizen participation and influence are perhaps greater in school districts than in any other unit of government in the United States. The most prominent institution of lay control is, of course, the school board. Over 90 percent of school board members are chosen by election, and the balance are appointed either by elected officials or by commissions named by elected officials. However chosen, the school board is a citizen legislative body with representative functions. The board appoints the superintendent and other administrators and may remove them. Legal authority flows from the public to the school board and from there to the school district administrators.

School districts offer unparalleled opportunites for direct citizen oversight and participation in policymaking. Important decisions are made at school board meetings held in the local community and open to the public. Public participation is solicited; many school boards hold regular public hearings to receive input from their constituents. Most school boards have standing and ad hoc committees, some of whose members are selected from the general public. In most school districts a citizen can reach school board members and top administrators, including superintendents, by telephone. More so than in other governments, the channels of citizen access to policymakers in school districts are numerous, convenient, and open.

Yet, in spite of the potential for lay control of education, the reality is quite different. The quantity and quality of citizen participation in local school governance are low. The superintendent and other professional administrators consistently dominate the public and the lay school board, regardless of the arena or the issue. Educational professionals control policy in local school districts because, democratic appearances notwithstanding, the institutions and procedural norms of school governance inhibit the influence of the lay public and promote the authority of professionals.

Professional Hegemony

The current institutional and behavioral norms of local educational governance are products of the municipal reform movement of the early twentieth century. It is possible to view the reform movement as a reaction against the excesses of a period with too much citizen control. Educational governance under political machines was responsive to citizen preferences but was also extremely corrupt. Reformers saw mass citizen participation and government corruption as causally related and sought to eliminate both.

Municipal and school reformers were guided by the same tripartite ideology: a general public interest should prevail over competing, partial interests; the public interest can be identified by the "best men," who should be given authority over government; and administration—the coordination of activities necessary to achieve the public interest—should be delegated to a corps of skilled professionals. Thus, educational reformers advocated institutional arrangements guaranteeing that those whom they regarded as the best candidates would be elected to school board positions and providing for professional educational managers to shoulder the burden of implementing policy decisions.

It is reasonable to argue that reformers were more successful in achieving their institutional goals in school districts than in municipal governments. Approximately half the municipalities in the United States employ the council-manager form of government, but virtually all school districts employ this form, i.e., a superintendent-board. Similarly, a greater proportion of school districts than municipalities have adopted electoral mechanisms that maximize the probability that the reformers' "best men" will be elected to the school board. About 75 percent of school boards are elected on a nonpartisan basis and about 75 percent on an at-large basis, and most school districts hold their elections when there are no state or federal elections. As a result, voter turnout for school district elections is typically low—on the order of 15 to 30 percent of the eligible electorate. Moreover, the turnout conforms with the reformers' notions of who should vote—individuals with greater than average wealth, education, and social and occupational status.

The patterns of participation in school district elections are reflected in the composition of school boards. School board members have the qualities that are esteemed in American society and that, according to reformers, qualify individuals to oversee local government. More often than not, they are male, white, middle-aged, long-time residents of their communities, well educated, engaged in prestigious occupations, Protestant, devout, and Republican. The upper-class bias of school boards is hardly unique; indeed, all elected bodies exhibit such a bias. What is unique is the isolation of school board members from political involvement. Board members are no more likely than the general public to come from homes involved in public affairs. The usual pattern of political elites with strong political backgrounds does not apply to them.

Adding to the upper-class, apolitical biases of school boards is the noncompetitive nature of the recruitment process and the strong tendency of boards to perpetuate themselves. School board elections are only moderately competitive. Most school board members can cite only one difference with their electoral opponents, and such differences usually do not relate directly to educational programs. Approximately 25 percent of school board members face no electoral competition. The average rate of incumbent electoral defeat is 34 percent.

In addition to perpetuation by default, there is deliberate self-perpetuation. About 25 percent of school board members who serve on elective boards originally gained their seats by appointment. It is not unusual for board members who are not seeking reelection to resign with a few months remaining in their terms of office to allow their colleagues to handpick a successor. The appointed member then enjoys the electoral advantages of incumbency in the election. If one adds the recruitment activity of the PTA, superintendents, and teachers to the recruitment activity of the board, about one-half of school board members are the products of self-perpetuation. Recruitment of other locally elected officials, such as city council members, exhibits many of the same patterns of self-perpetuation.

School board members tend to be drawn from the professional and managerial classes of society. Through training and experience they have developed expertise in their businesses and professions, but they defer to the expertise of professional educational administrators. Moreover, their school board associations tell them to accede to administrative judgment:

> School directors are not trained in the technical aspects of school administration. They select an executive officer—the superintendent—who has such training. It is that person's responsibility to advise the board on sound educational procedures. . . .
> It is agreed by authorities in the field of educational administration that the legislation of policies is the most important function of the school board and that the execution of these policies should be left wholly to the professional expert, the superinten-

dent of schools. Boards of education do not have the time to execute their policies, nor do they usually have the technical training needed for such work.[1]

Administrators are trained to expect such deference and to take the policy initiative at all times. The original reform division of labor between school boards (policymaking) and superintendents (administration) has been lost. Most school board members today do not view themselves as representatives communicating constituent preferences to administrators. They view their tasks as legitimizing decisions made by administrators, publicizing administrative decisions, and generating public support for those policies.

Thus, it should come as no surprise that about two-thirds of school boards delegate the agenda-setting function solely to administrators. A recent study by the authors of communications and decision-making in school districts found that three-fourths of all items considered by school boards at public meetings were discussed at the initiative of the superintendent and his staff. Not all discussions were intended to result in formal decisions, yet explicit administrative policy recommendations were made in nearly two-thirds of school board discussions. Administrative recommendations were adopted in 99 percent of decisions made by formal vote, and nearly 85 percent of school board votes were unanimous. School board members did as they were told.

The public enters the process after the issues have been defined. Public attendance at school board meetings is generally low and concentrated in a few meetings during the year. Widespread public attendance and participation usually follow a major decision. On the average, public comment is heard in about 20 percent of school board meetings. About 10 percent of statements at the meetings are made by those outside the educational establishment.

Not only is the quantity of public input low, but the quality is also. Less than 40 percent of public statements express policy preferences. Most citizens who speak at school board meetings are simply seeking or supplying information. Most public expressions of policy preferences are in support of administrative proposals. Although the quality of interactions between school officials and citizens in nonpublic settings is higher (more than half of such communications articulate policy preferences), the quantity is low. The typical superintendent reported five private citizen contacts a week; the typical school board member reported three a month.

Given the relative infrequency of direct citizen preference articulation, one might speculate that the few who do participate exercise considerable influence. Such is not the case. Lay policy requests made at school board meetings are rarely met with a timely, responsive decision. Constituent demands serve to place an issue on the school board's policy agenda. Decisions are made weeks or months later, after administrators have had time to make a policy recommendation.

Citizen requests made in private communications are generally more

[1] Washington State School Directors' Association, *Boardsmanship* (Olympia, Washington: Washington State School Directors' Association, 1975), pp. 6.1–6.2.

moderate in tone and in scope of necessary action than demands made at school board meetings. The typical constituent demand made at a school board meeting is for the board to make a certain decision, while the typical private request is for an individual school official to take a certain course of action, such as referring a problem to the school board or an appropriate administrator. Yet less than 40 percent of school official-constituent private interactions result in the school official's taking the action requested. Moreover, school officials report that they are not influenced by more than half of constituent private communications and more than two-thirds of constituent public presentations. Thus the articulate minority usually do not exercise influence over school district officials and rarely achieve policy goals as a direct result of their participation. The reform goal of insulating school district governance from mass citizen participation and influence has been well met.

Control in Perspective

On the surface, the social and political turbulence of the past decade seems to have contributed to a politicization of local educational governance. Popular accounts of highly publicized conflicts have portrayed professionals as struggling vainly against a variety of powerful lay forces. Professionals themselves have been active in promulgating the view that local school district administrators have become beleaguered with conflict. One administrator has said, "The American school superintendent, long the benevolent ruler whose word was law, has become a harried, embattled figure of waning authority. . . . Brow-beaten by once subservient boards of education, [teachers' associations], and parents, the superintendent can hardly be blamed if he feels he has lost control of his destiny. . . . Administrative powerlessness is becoming one of the most pervasive realities of organizational life."[2] While some might be inclined to dismiss such testimony as self-serving, the view has been to some extent echoed by scholars who argue that professional dominance no longer characterizes local school governance.

The dominance of local administrators may also be threatened by collective bargaining agreements with teachers' unions. The primary foci of such agreements, which now govern more than half of the nation's public school teachers, are salaries and working conditions. Teachers are increasingly arguing for an expansion of negotiable working conditions and are demanding representation on bodies that set curricular policy, select textbooks, recommend educational programs, and evaluate teachers. Since collective bargaining agreements are viewed as personnel matters, negotiations are conducted in private. Public disclosure of bargaining positions or strategies is an unfair labor practice. Thus, while collective bargaining may lead to a redistribution of influence among members of the local educational establishment, it is unlikely to increase the influence of the lay public or school board.

[2] Donald A. Erickson, "Moral Dilemmas of Administrative Powerlessness," *Administrators' Notebook* (April 1972), pp. 3–4.

It is true that in any given year some school districts will experience episodes of conflict because of lay participation. It is also true that some districts, principally large urban districts that must cater to heterogeneous populations, have a significant minority of dissatisfied and vocal lay clients. Nevertheless, overall, laymen rarely participate in school governance. Moreover, professional administrators dominate the decision-making process in virtually all cases in which there is substantial lay participation.

This is not to say that students and practitioners of educational administration are acting in bad faith when they complain of the dangers of political conflict in education. If one believes, as they do, that mass lay participation and school board refusal to accept professional recommendations under any circumstances are pathological, then any amount of such conflict is unacceptable. School districts are not philosophically or institutionally prepared to accept conflict as a normal aspect of governance. Thus conflict episodes, though rare, are momentous.

In the long run, the power of local educational professionals may well be threatened by educational professionals in state and federal governments. Their options may be circumscribed by state and federal courts, state and federal economic problems, and other forces originating outside the local school district that are beyond their control. The power of local educational professionals will not be strongly threatened by school boards or by the lay public within the local school district so long as the norms and institutions of educational governance insulate educational policymaking from politics.

Educational Accountability

Citizen dissatisfaction with the schools, fueled by rapidly rising school costs and declining student achievement test scores during the last decade, has catalyzed a contemporary campaign to establish a new balance between lay and professional control. This contemporary effort, popularly known as the "accountability movement," derives its energy from a large and diverse political circle, including fiscal conservatives, ethnic and racial minorities, alienated and antibureaucratic liberals, disappointed parents, and frustrated citizens. The diversity found in this group has resulted in imprecise terms and labels, fragmented legislative objectives, spasmodic campaign activities, and erratic political alliances. On occasion, reformers focus their efforts on the revision of federal programs; just as frequently they attempt to have their objectives included in state statutes or local school district policy. To add to the complexity, the accountability movement frequently has a faddish air that many professional educators and some state officals have hoped would go away.

Despite the confusion accompanying the accountability movement, there are reasons to believe that at least some of its consequences will be long lasting and thus deserve description and analysis. The purpose of this essay is to examine the accountability movement's roots, describe its current manifestations, and reach some understanding of its future legacy.

Interaction among three major values—equality, efficiency, and liberty—has influenced public school policy in the United States for at least two centuries. Practical steps necessary to implement these values usually conflict with one another, such as elite versus egalitarian entrance standards and local property taxes versus strong state financial equalization. Consequently, public school policies generally represent a compromise between existing values. Occasionally, however, a particular value will enjoy a period of public ascendancy sufficiently strong to shape a policy era. This has been the case with the concern for efficiency at least three times during the history of United States public schools.

The concern with efficiency first mounted during the midnineteenth century and focused on the adoption of European teaching methods for American schools. The second period began at the turn of the twentieth century and lasted for approximately twenty-five years, and this movement is worthy of extended discussion because the contemporary accountability effort exists as a substantial counterreaction to the efficiency reforms begun half a century earlier.

The coincidence of three reform movements in the early 1900s resulted in an era of school governance that was characterized as the "Cult of Efficiency." The muckrakers uncovered political scandal not only in municipal circles but also in school governance. The evils of illegal contracts, rebates, nepotism, and the spoils system were attributed to an excess of politics. The obvious solution was to insulate school governance from the partisan political process. This principle had two practical effects, the dilution of lay control and citizen participation in school decisions and the promotion of professionalized school managers. Lay control was altered by such methods as declaring school board positions to be appointive or listed as nonpartisan on the ballot, changing the times of school elections so as not to coincide with municipal elections, eliminating ward school boards and creating highly visible central boards in cities, providing teachers with tenure, demanding competitive bids for the purchase of goods and services, and granting school districts their own taxing authority. This latter condition was intended to render school boards fiscally independent of the scandal-ridden city machines that the body politic considered threatening.

Actions taken to separate schools from partisan politics proved extraordinarily successful. School policy declined significantly not only as a topic of partisan debate but also as an issue of general public interest. School decisions were becoming both geographically and politically remote from citizens. This insulation took place during a time when many school districts were undergoing a substantial increase in enrollment. The combination of Progressive Era reforms and population expansion contributed to the creation of centralized school systems and managerial hierarchies. This trend toward bureaucracy coincided with a private sector management revolution stressing efficiency, and the confluence of the two movements greatly furthered the growth of professional school administrators.

During the nineteenth century, school board members typically made policy and acted as executive officers. A management layer between school boards and teachers seldom existed. Toward the end of the century, New York and a few other large eastern cities employed professional school superintendents. Management tasks had outstripped the time, energy, and expertise of lay board members. This trend was reinforced not only by the centralization reforms already described but also by fascination in the private sector with "scientific management." This was the era of efficiency experts and time and motion analysts. If business could be professionalized, so could schools. "Scientifically" oriented school management experts would bring a new era of productivity into education. If they also assisted in making schools apolitical, so much the better.

"Scientific" administration ultimately proved to be not very scientific and relatively ineffective in solving school problems. Nevertheless, the inflated level of middle management that it spawned still persists. This central management is widely criticized by the contemporary efficiency advocates as a major barrier to accountability, because it buffers schools from their clients. But it is seldom taken into account that middle management's major function has changed so that it is occupied primarily with ensuring local compliance with state and federal accountability requirements.

Not only did the scientific management movement stimulate production of "expert" school administrators, but it also triggered a nationwide wave of school and school district consolidations. The new breed of school managers, eager to display their scientific prowess and their concern for public-sector efficiency, recommended that small schools be closed and that rural districts be collapsed into larger units. They argued that larger units would save dollars and provide better educational opportunities. It was difficult to challenge the new professionals and their counterparts in the private sector. Rural residents resisted, but their position ultimately paled when confronted with consolidation's twin benefits of economy and better service.

Thus, both in cities and in the countryside, schools and school districts became larger, more bureaucratized, professionally managed, and insulated from the public. This was the state of affairs by the end of the 1920s. Any negative public reaction was drowned by the problems of the next three decades—financial depression, international war, and unmatched population growth.

Not until the 1960s did sufficient stability exist to examine the reform era's consequences. However, when the first antibureaucracy reforms did come, they were not intended to benefit the public. By this time, the bureaucratization of school management had contributed to a sense of inefficacy on the part of teachers. If they could no longer deal directly as individuals with school board members, and if they were to be subjected to lists of standardized rules promulgated by central office managers, they could at least attempt to retain a degree of dignity by forming professional unions and engaging in collective bargaining. By this process, teachers hoped once again to shape directly the decisions that affected their working lives.

On balance the goals of unionization were achieved; teacher collective bargaining is now formally or informally possible throughout the United States. One of the outcomes, however, was to dilute public control even further. Whatever the assets of collective bargaining for teachers, students, and society, it also necessitates the sharing of decision-making authority with the unions. While board members usually are elected officials, teacher union representatives are not similarly accountable to the public. Consequently, by the beginning of the 1970s schools appeared substantially beyond the reach of direct public control. Fifty years of well-intentioned reform efforts were increasingly perceived by informed citizens as having created a system that should be held accountable for its actions.

The Contemporary Accountability Movement

Tracing the roots of social or political reform can entail an almost infinite regress. Suffice it to say that several major conditions appeared to coalesce during the late 1960s and early 1970s to constitute the contemporary accountability movement. These conditions included the previously described dilution of public authority and ascendancy of professional control over education, the rapid escalation of school costs, and a perceived decline in school productivity. The last two conditions especially deserve elaboration.

According to the U.S. Office of Education, the average annual per-pupil expenditure for public schools in 1940 was $100. By 1976–77 this figure had increased to more than $1,500. Even when inflation is taken into account, per-pupil growth in school costs exceeded 500 percent. In the aggregate, by 1975, schools were absorbing approximately $80 billion annually, approximately half of which was generated locally from property taxes. Moreover, these revenue figures displayed little prospect of declining, or even stabilizing, despite the fact that public school enrollments reached their peak in 1971 and have been declining in each subsequent year.

During the late 1960s and early 1970s—when escalating school costs were drawing publicity—student achievement, as measured by relatively objective means such as Scholastic Aptitude Tests (SAT) and the National Assessment of Education Progress (NAEP), began to decline. Professional educators offered various explanations intended to shelter schools from blame. A prestigious national commission, chaired by a former secretary of labor, Willard Wirtz, undertook an exhaustive examination of the issue and reported that the blame resided with society generally and a few school practices in particular. Aside from the validity of the commission's findings, it is not altogether clear that such explanations mattered. For the growing number of accountability advocates, the simplest linkage sufficed; schools were not doing their job.

Whatever its immediate causes, the contemporary effort to gain greater accountability first emerged in the late 1960s. For the next decade almost all of the educational world resounded with the catch phrases of productivity, such as systems analysis, zero-based budgeting, competency-based teaching, program performance budgeting, and management by objectives. The movement's initial decade appears to have had two major dimensions. One was an effort to revamp the governance structure of schools and to encourage citizen participation and lay control. The second strategy attempted to apply a variety of technocratic procedures to enhance school productivity. Though by no means exhausted, these efforts may have reached their peak.

Neither the political nor the technocratic strategy shows promise of substantial success, and accountability advocates may adopt different strategies for their efforts during the next ten years. These alternative accountability dimensions are considerably more drastic than their immediate predecessors. One involves the imposition of spending limits on government in general and schools in particular. Its advocates say, "If we cannot gain greater school productivity, then we can at least reduce the drain on the taxpayer's purse." The second possible new strategy seeks a dramatic alteration in the governance structure for schools. By the use of vouchers, the educational consumer would become the prime decision-maker in education and would utilize Adam Smith's "invisible hand" to promote greater accountability.

Accountability Strategies

A series of publications in 1966 and 1967, aimed at decentralizing New York City's schools, marked the beginning of the political accountability strategy. These reports, the most significant of which were sponsored by a major foundation, suggested that New York City's mammoth school system, serving more than a million students, could be rendered effective only through substantial decentralization. The reports immediately became controversial, sponsors quickly offered disclaimers, and the prime author eventually sought new employment.

Whatever their shortcomings, these publications rapidly became the marching orders for New York City's school reformers. Frustrated by their inability to pierce the hegemony of teacher unions, professional school administrators, and a distant central city school board, they demanded "community control" over their children's schools. These demands precipitated substantial conflict between professional educators and other defenders of the status quo on one hand and vocal community activists and minority groups on the other.

The eventual result was disappointing to the activists. Three limited community control "experiments" were permitted, but only for a short time, and they became embroiled in heated charges of anti-Semitism. They were closed when opponents objected to them on grounds such as rampant disregard for conventional personnel procedures. The New York State Legislature ultimately responded to the furor by mandating the reconstitution of the city's elementary and junior high schools into thirty-one separate districts each having a popularly elected board of education. Community control proponents were quick to point to the inefficiency involved in creating subunits, each of which contained a population approximately the size of Syracuse. Moreover, cynics claimed that the initial school board elections only displayed the teachers' ability to manipulate the system to elect local board candidates sympathetic to their views. Even then, these community boards were subject to the final authority of the central board.

Aside from its reality, New York's community control movement was important for its rhetoric. It generated nationwide discussion of the issue of citizen participation in school decisions. Other urban districts followed the New York City example and undertook some version of decentralization. More frequently than not, this involved dividing the city into three or four administrative subunits, which seldom resulted in greater lay control.

The federal government and several states were similarly influenced by the attention given to the need for greater citizen participation. Citizen advisory councils and school-site parent councils gained in popularity. Two major federal programs, the Elementary and Secondary Education Act of 1965 (ESEA) and the Emergency School Aid Act of 1972 (ESAA) were amended during the early 1970s to mandate parent councils in the local schools and school districts receiving federal funds. At the state level, Florida led the way by adopting in

1972 a comprehensive reform plan that employed the school site, with a parent advisory council, as a basic component of educational governance.

Both federal and state efforts to invoke greater citizen participation were predicated on the assumption that increased lay control would assist in making educators more accountable. This control was moderated to avoid the excesses of politics that had characterized the schools during the muckraking era. The reforms of the 1970s were designed to balance professional and citizen interests. Critics were quick to point out that the new participation procedures were impotent, granting no authentic decision-making power whatsoever to lay people. Moreover, they alleged that the new citizen councils were easily co-opted by teachers and administrators. For their part, professional educators chided council members for meddling and not understanding the distinction between policymaking or advising on the one hand and administration and practice on the other. In short, this was an attempt to socialize the new participants to a limited view of their role. Also, elected board members at the school district level were not altogether comfortable with school site councils that threatened to limit their own decision-making powers.

There are few empirical studies regarding the effectiveness of this effort to repoliticize schools. Whether lay participation has resulted in added lay control and greater accountability is not known. Regardless of the success of this reform strategy, however, it left unsatisfied another large category of accountability proponents—those who desired a more technical approach to the problem of school productivity.

Publicly expressed desires for added technical efficiency in schools may have been initiated with the Sputnik-inspired curriculum efforts of the early 1960s to introduce the "new" math and science to education. More explicit demands for adopting modern management and technical procedures by schools burgeoned almost a decade later, around 1970. Management devices such as systems analysis, management by objectives (MBO), program evaluation and review techniques (PERT), and program performance budgeting systems (PPBS) had been honed during World War II, polished in the private sector during the postwar period, and rose to their greatest prominence with the space program successes of the 1960s. If these new procedures could help put a man on the moon, surely they could assist in teaching youngsters to read.

The application of modern management techniques to increase accountability initially concentrated on inputs, then on school processes, and finally began to focus out of desperation on the product of schooling—student achievement. Efforts to understand the effects of school inputs are well illustrated by a 1966 study, *Equal Educational Opportunity*, better known as the Coleman report. Its major author, James S. Coleman, and his research colleagues attempted a complicated statistical search for the correlates of student achievement. In a set of intensely publicized findings they stated that few school effects were independent of a student's social class and neighborhood. The press and lay audiences widely interpreted this fact to mean that additional funds for schools did not affect student learning; books, science laboratories, new buildings, counselors, and small classes were only costly trappings. The authentic antecedents of achievements were to be found in the home and neighborhood.

If accountability proponents could not specify what resource mix every school should utilize in order to achieve optimum productivity, then they could at least stress the "correct" processes that teachers should use in instructing pupils. This led to a wave of national conferences and state statutes on competency based teacher education (CBTE). The idea was a simple one in the abstract. Teachers should be taught procedures that enabled them to be effective instructors. Once they had mastered this set of professional techniques, then they could be certified as competent and licensed to teach. The plan suffered from one major flaw and proved to be a fad. Despite the exaggerated promises of teacher trainers, the scientific basis for pedagogy was simply too thin to permit competency-based training. There was no set of specific teacher behaviors that consistently led to student achievement. It rapidly became evident that teaching still remained far more of an art than a science. CBTE died quickly in most states, and accountability proponents attempted one last technocratic attack on the problem of school productivity by specifying and measuring student outcomes.

Employers complained about and national test scores confirmed the fact that high school graduates were distressingly undereducated. A high school diploma had become meaningless. Schools had to return to a period of rigor, graduation standards needed to be elevated, and parents, employers, and taxpayers needed to know what quality of schooling they were obtaining for their tax money. The solution that developed for this problem was the imposition of minimum competency standards for successful high school graduation. Florida instituted such a statewide program in 1975. By 1978, thirty-four states had a similar requirement. In twenty states graduation was contingent on passing a competency examination. In the remaining fourteen states, course requirements for graduation were increased and made more specific, and the standard for passing was increased.

The minimum competency concept drew its largest support from the business community. Business representatives argued that schooling should be "results oriented"; activities should be consistent with organizational objectives; increasing the bottom line is ultimately what counts. It follows from such reasoning that measures of productivity, such as student achievement, are crucial.

Teacher organizations were prime opponents of such competency standards. They contended that the goals of schooling were much too complicated and subtle to be measured by pencil and paper tests using so-called objective questions. Such mechanisms could never capture important school outcomes such as "appreciation for individual differences," "elimination of racial stereotypes," and "growth in self-respect." Worse yet, opponents contended, was the tendency of easily measured school objectives to force subtleties out of the curriculum. Schooling would produce only intellectual results; students would be feelingless robots incapable of appreciating deeper values.

Teacher organizations politically opposed implementation of such standards in state legislatures. They also filed suits questioning the legality of minimum competency tests and gained the support of several minority group organizations that resented the racially disproportionate burden of failure that competency examinations threatened to impose. Teachers' political opposition served to dilute competency requirements in many states, but the movement had too much momentum to be halted altogether. Court decisions have been too mixed to predict their final impact. Regardless of the legislative success of competency proponents, however, no dramatic reversal in student performance appears to have occurred. Consequently, some dissatisfied accountability advocates remain willing to attempt one or both of two remaining strategies —revenue limits and vouchers.

The highly progressive income tax structures of the federal government and many states, coupled with inflation in residential property values, incited substantial tax resistance in the 1970s. California's Proposition 13 enacted in 1978 was among the most highly visible examples of this phenomenon, but it was by no means a bizarre exception. (Even in California, the growth in school revenues had begun to decrease six years before Proposition 13.) An increasingly popular legislative solution was to impose revenue or expenditure ceilings on the government, local government and education, as well as state governments.

Efforts to control government costs are promoted by many fiscally conservative interests. Among them are those who utilize school costs as an example of public-sector waste. Throughout Howard Jarvis's 1978 California campaign in behalf of Proposition 13, he consistently drew the most favorable audience response when he attacked schools for being little more than baby-sitting agencies. The general rationale among a segment of the electorate was that if added school productivity could not somehow be induced, then at least a limit could be placed on the amount of public money available for educators to waste. The greatest opposition to such limitations has come from teachers and other groups of public employees. Aside from protecting their self-interests, these opponents contend that the public's long-run welfare will be impaired by reductions in school spending.

While added political participation, greater technocratic control, and revenue ceilings can come and go, there remains an even more radical group of accountability proponents who do not necessarily oppose any of the other three strategies but find them all too timid. They advocate a voucher system, a reform that would vest school decision-making in the home. A government warrant redeemable only for school services would be granted parents for each child. They would select the school of their choice, which would then operate from the revenues obtained through such vouchers. Dissatisfied parents would be free to select another school.

Voucher advocates contend that the imposition of market pressures would render schools more sensitive to client preferences, enormously less bureaucratic, and thus more efficient. Voucher opponents argue that regardless of whatever added efficiency such plans portend, they offer a dangerous threat to social cohesion and would even more seriously violate the First Amendment's "establishment of religion clause."

Vouchers have been used in the United States for government support of higher education. With the exception of an insignificant experiment in one California district, however, vouchers have not been tried for public lower education. To date, a powerful coalition of public school interest groups, such as teachers, administrators, and school board members, has successfully opposed voucher proposals at the state and federal level. Increased congressional interest in tuition tax credit bills may reflect growing public willingness to accept a voucher plan. Voucher proponents believe that many of the previous attempts to achieve accountability, particularly revenue limitations, will so disrupt public schools that during the 1980s the electorate will turn to voucher plans as the way to rescue the nation's education system.

Accountability's Legacy

The present accountability movement is still too young to permit an easy assessment of its long-lasting consequences. Neither the political nor technocratic strategy appears to have had dramatic success in elevating student achievement or reducing school costs. Perhaps their results take longer to appear. If in time more citizens participate in school decisions, that by itself may be a useful outcome. The movement will also prove beneficial if competency standards encourage teachers and administrators to stress skills considered important by the larger society. Conversely, if added citizen involvement leads either to the scandalous excesses of half a century ago or merely impedes instruction, then it will have been a hollow effort. Similarly, if competency standards eventually result in uniformly mediocre schools wherein the minimum also becomes the maximum, it too will have been an abortive reform.

Revenue ceilings could lead to more efficient use of school resources while student achievement remains stable or increases. As for the fourth strategy, if all else fails to enhance puplic support for and trust in schools, then vouchers may indeed be the final avenue of hope. In the process, however, extraordinary attention must be given to the possibility of dysfunctional social segregation.

No social reform seems to be beneficial forever. The changes to schools undertaken in the Progressive Era—depoliticization, school consolidation, and professionalized administrators—were motivated by the best of intentions. These very reforms, however, sowed the seeds for school accountability problems half a century later. Thus it is difficult to refute Emerson's argument that "every reform is only a mask under cover of which a more terrible reform, which dares not yet name itself, advances."

Organized Teachers
and Local Schools

LORRAINE M. MCDONNELL
ANTHONY H. PASCAL

Traditionally, public school teachers were viewed as an apolitical group who defined their interests no differently from school administrators and local boards of education. In the last fifteen years, however, that image has changed radically. Not only has the advent of teacher collective bargaining awakened a new militancy in teachers, but support of electoral candidates and legislative lobbying have led to their emergence as a powerful political force. Now school management often finds itself in open conflict with organized teachers.

Both the American Federation of Teachers (AFT) and the National Education Association (NEA), with a combined membership of over 2 million teachers, have chosen a dual strategy in order to obtain greater economic and status benefits for their members. On the one hand, local AFT and NEA affiliates now bargain collectively not only over wages, fringe benefits, and working conditions but also over professional items such as teacher participation in textbook selection and curriculum development. According to the U.S. Census Bureau, formal collective bargaining agreements covered 60 percent of all public school teachers by 1975.

Organized teachers also engage in widespread political activity. Both the AFT and the NEA recognize the real limits on the gains attainable through local-level collective bargaining. Consequently, these organizations have chosen to commit considerable resources to lobbying and support for political candidates. In 1976, NEA expenditures on behalf of Jimmy Carter exceeded $400,000. In addition, over $3 million was spent by local and state affiliates. Although the AFT only spent a total of about $400,000 on the 1976 campaign, its parent, the AFL-CIO, raised several million dollars for political candidates. Similar efforts were repeated at the state and local levels. For example, the political action arm of the California Teachers Association spent more than $550,000 in the 1974 election. In fact, only the oil industry spent more than the AFT and the NEA in that California election.

While this combination of collective bargaining and political action is a relatively new strategy, lobbying by teacher organizations is not. Prior to collective bargaining, lobbying by state teacher organizations accounted for most of the economic and job security benefits teachers obtained. Tenure and continuing-contract laws, statewide, joint-contributory retirement plans, and the minimum salary standards established by some states all resulted from legislative action by organized teachers.

However, there is now a difference. A teacher organization can first attempt to obtain a specific benefit at the bargaining table. If it fails at this level, it can bypass the local board of education and lobby at the state level. Here the teacher organization often finds itself trying to persuade legislators whom it has itself helped to elect. The potential for enormous influence is obvious.

Many feel that organized teachers have profoundly altered the patterns of governance in public education. David Tyack, in his history of American urban education, has argued that while power was lodged in small boards and powerful superintendents at the turn of the century, today teachers as a group have the greatest power to veto or sabotage proposals for reform. No realistic estimate of strategies for change in American education can afford to ignore teachers or fail to enlist their support.[1]

Local school board members charge that organized teachers have usurped the boards' policymaking authority. Some school managers use even stronger terms in describing the effect of organized teachers. For example, a past president of the Alabama Association of School Administrators asserted: "Educators are being steered by selfish, empire-building and power-mad union teachers down a stream of no return, a stream that is guaranteed to divide the educational ranks, to set the public against us and turn the control of our educational system over to teacher unions that are not subject to public accountability, yet have the power to bring education to a **halt**."[2]

To what extent are these charges valid? Have organized teachers really become the new power elite in education? Have local boards of education lost significant influence to teachers through collective bargaining?

As part of a research project sponsored by the National Institute of Education, a Rand Corporation team examined these issues in one of the first empirical studies of the noneconomic effects of teacher collective bargaining.[3] The study had two main objectives: to determine the effect of collective bargaining on school and classroom practices and to assess its impact on school and district-level decision-making.

---

[1] David B. Tyack, *The One Best System* (Cambridge: Harvard University Press, 1974), pp. 288-89.

[2] Tom James, "Seeking the Limits of Bargaining," *Compact* 9 (June 1975): 13.

[3] The authors wish to thank Dennis Doyle, David Mandel, and Marc Tucker of NIE for their support throughout this project. The following Rand consultants and staff members are also gratefully acknowledged for their contributions: Charles Cheng, Jane Cobb, Barbra Davis, Larry Day, Renee Gould, Marjorie Green, Meg Gwaltney, William Lisowski, Ellen Marks, Susan Reese, Abby Robyn, Richard Victor, Joanne Wuchitech, and Gail Zellman.

A national random sample of 155 teacher contracts was examined for 1970 and again for 1975 to determine exactly what types of provisions had been included and how they differed over time and across types of school districts. Analysts undertook fieldwork in fifteen of these districts, selected on the basis of the factors found important in the analysis of the contracts. While in the field the following topics were explored: the way the collective bargaining process operates, the extent to which collective bargaining gains are institutionalized by local teacher organizations, and whether political action is used to supplement bargaining outcomes. The analysis indicates that the results for organized teachers have been mixed.

Collective Bargaining Gains

Defining an appropriate scope of bargaining is one of the knottiest problems in labor negotiations and particularly so for teachers. In the private sector the National Labor Relations Board has limited the topics of mandatory bargaining to wages, hours, and working conditions. When applied to teacher collective bargaining, this narrow delineation has generated ambiguity and conflict. Central are the practical difficulties in making a clear-cut distinction between working conditions and matters of educational policy. For example, is class size a working condition or a policy issue?

Teachers' own notions of professionalism further complicate the definition of scope, because they expect to play a larger role in defining their work standards than would nonprofessional employees. Based on this notion of professionalism, teachers have demanded a larger voice in educational decisions and more control over the implementation of educational programs. Organized teachers argue that as professionals they have superior training in the specifics of the learning process than do most policymakers and can therefore more knowledgeably make those decisions that most directly affect the classroom environment. Consequently, the bargaining agendas of local teacher organizations have often included demands for teacher participation in curriculum design, staff evaluation procedures, and student discipline and grading practices. Obviously, some of these items require local school districts to increase their expenditures. More important, many school board members fear that these demands represent a fundamental challenge to managerial authority. The Rand research indicates that organized teachers have successfully negotiated a number of provisions that have constrained the traditional prerogatives of school management. These gains, however, have been neither universal nor total. Table 1 shows, for the sample of 155 school districts, the fraction that had negotiated each of eleven key provisions into teacher contracts by 1970 and by 1975. Only four provisions—grievance arbitration, class hours, pupil exclusion, and teacher evaluation—were included in a majority of teacher contracts by 1975.

Organized teachers seek strong grievance provisions early in the bargaining relationship. They realize that the grievance procedure lies at the "heart of the

TABLE 1

Percentage of Contracts Containing Key Provisions

Key Provision	Attained by 1970	Attained between 1970 and 1975
All grievances to be subject to arbitration	80%	10%
Minimum number of aides per classroom specified	12	14
Maximum class size specified	23	10
Maximum class hours specified	50	20
Teachers can exclude a disruptive pupil	32	18
An instructional policy committee to be established	18	11
Teachers can respond formally to evaluation	38	13
Teachers can refuse assignment	14	11
Only seniority and credentials to determine promotion	23	3
Involuntary transferees to be selected on specific criteria	26	10
Reduction-in-force procedures spelled out	13	31

Source: Rand Corporation.
Note: Based on a national random sample of 155 teacher contracts.

contract" and that the operational effectiveness of all other provisions hinges on it. For want of a grievance provision, a broad contract with many provisions may be emasculated in practice. At the same time, school management often accepts a strong grievance procedure, with third party arbitration, since it minimizes labor-management conflict and fosters productive relations between the two parties.

The number of class hours is a working condition clearly within the traditional scope of bargaining and has gained acceptance by most employers. Pupil exclusion and teacher evaluation, however, constitute much more professionally oriented items, although these provisions do not limit the flexibility of school boards or the central administration. Rather, they constrain the latitude of school-site principals. The Rand analysts found that school boards often acquiesce to teacher demands that compromise the authority of school-site management and resist those that limit the board's own prerogatives. To some extent, principals command the least leverage in collective bargaining. Although ostensibly part of the district's management team, they are often isolated from the district's decision-making process. On the other hand, teacher collective bargaining has severely weakened the traditional community of interest between teachers and principals, who have in some cases become adversaries.

Only a minority of the contracts included provisions on teacher assignment, promotion, and transfer, largely because school management resisted their inclusion. Where teachers did succeed in attaining such provisions, school board members and superintendents complained about the constriction these items placed on their own policymaking roles. The field research turned up extremes in these provisions as in others. For example, in one district the teacher organization wields effective veto over all administrative promotions through its contractually mandated participation on a screening committee. But that is clearly a deviant and extreme case. In most contracts with promotion, assignment, and transfer items, seniority and credentials tend to comprise the criteria. Yet even these constrain management by effectively preventing the assignment of teachers on the basis of an administrator's judgment of performance and suitability for a specific position.

Teacher organizations often demand contractual provisions as a reaction to institutional forces external to the school district. For example, the extraordinary increase in the inclusion of reduction-in-force provisions stems from the major shift in student enrollment after 1970. With more and more school districts facing enrollment declines and financial constraints, teacher organizations moved to establish formal criteria for teacher layoffs.

Items may also appear in an organization's bargaining agenda because of state and federal directives. The federal Education for All Handicapped Children Act of 1975 (PL 94–142) includes such mandates. In the majority of districts the Rand team visited, school and teacher organization officials reported that the requirements of PL 94–142 had become a subject of bargaining. Many teacher organizations, in response to their national affiliates, are demanding released time to prepare individualized education programs, extra weight in computing class size for handicapped students who are mainstreamed into regular classrooms, and adequate in-service education to handle mainstreamed students. Judicial rulings requiring racially balanced school faculties have raised the saliency of criteria for involuntary teacher transfers. Still other state and federal programs mandate parent-teacher advisory councils that have implications for such contract items as length of the teacher's workday, time spent with parents, and the role of teachers in school decision-making.

In responding to external pressures, teacher organizations have not only tried to protect their contracts but have also worked to accommodate these mandates. For example, in one desegregating district the teacher organization negotiated a lottery system to assign teachers to the new cluster schools. District administrators and teachers agreed that this negotiated system made the process smoother and more equitable. In other districts, teachers agreed to exclude some teacher hiring, promotion, and transfer issues from contractual seniority criteria so as to accommodate affirmative action objectives.

The study attempted to explain why certain provisions were included in some teacher contracts and not in others on the basis of district demographics and teacher organizational characteristics such as the group's strength and militancy. The research established, however, that the best predictor of whether a given provision was included in a contract lay in the state law regulating the scope of bargaining. Districts in states that permitted or mandated bargaining on a particular item were much more likely to have that contract provision than districts in states with more restrictive scopes of bargaining provisions.

Yet the existence of a favorable state statutory environment does not of itself guarantee that a provision will be included in a contract. The field studies showed that even in states with broad statutes, local political and organizational factors often prevail over the prescriptions of state law. For example, weak teacher organizations find it difficult to overcome the resistance of a strong board, despite advantages provided by a favorable state statute. Nevertheless, it is true that teacher organizations more easily obtain provisions in states where statutes permit a broad scope.

Where a statutory statewide agency oversees public employee labor relations, legislatures have seldom defined the scope of bargaining. Rather, they have left it to the regulatory agency to enumerate allowable items on a case-by-case basis. Where no state commission exists, the task of defining the scope of bargaining often falls to the courts, which frequently base their rulings on precedents established in the private sector. Such precedents have played a role, for example, in the determination of the status of class size as either a management prerogative or a working condition.

Increasingly, state legislatures have moved to limit or more clearly define the permissible scope of bargaining. New laws in Nevada, Indiana, and Montana list extensive management rights that strengthen the bargaining position of local school boards and place educational policy matters outside the scope of bargaining. In Pennsylvania, on the other hand, the legal scope of bargaining has become broader over time. There the state supreme court ruled that items related to the employees' interest in wages, hours, and conditions of employment fell within matters subject to good-faith bargaining, even though they might touch on managerial policy. This decision has meant that few items are excluded from the legal scope of bargaining. The role of the state law in determining the scope of bargaining will expand as more states consider public employee collective bargaining laws and as the debate over proposed federal legislation in this area continues.

Teachers have obviously made substantial gains through the collective bargaining process. They now have greater control over their workday and their classrooms. They increasingly influence district and school-site policies. Yet teacher influence varies greatly from district to district, and the teacher organization with an effective veto over school management is the rare exception. Many of the demands of organized teachers occur in response to initiatives originating from outside the local school district. In making these demands, teacher organizations in states with broad statutes fare better than their counterparts in states with restrictive statutes.

Teacher organizations realize that higher levels of government play a major role in determining collective bargaining outcomes. Factors external to the local context affect what teachers obtain at the bargaining table; the policies and processes of higher levels of government impose real limits on potential collective bargaining attainments. Consequently, teacher organizations have moved to supplement collective bargaining with political action.

Political Action

The two national teacher organizations, along with their state and local affiliates, engage intensively in political action at all three levels of government. They support candidates ranging from school board members to the president of the

United States. In conjunction with this electoral activity, the teacher organizations lobby to increase federal and state aid to education, to secure more advantageous public employee collective bargaining laws, and to achieve concrete advantages such as reduced class size.

In some instances, organized teachers use the political process to facilitate a favorable collective bargaining outcome for themselves. In fact, in a system of shared responsibility among branches and levels of government, public employee unions adopt strategies to exploit the division of authority. Variants on the basic strategy of bypassing or end-run bargaining abound. Essentially, bypassing is an attempt by employee organizations to use political pressure on elected officials to undermine the position of the management negotiator.

On the local level, a union may negotiate directly with a professional labor relations expert who represents the school board, while using political pressure on elected officials. In public education particularly, end-run bargaining sometimes consists of pressure on the mayor of a city to intervene in teacher disputes with the local school board. For example, in his study of public sector unionism in Philadelphia, F.J. Foley found that by threatening strike action the AFT-affiliate convinced the mayor to join negotiations and to provide the extra funds needed to reach a settlement.[4]

Another form of bypassing exploits the vertical sharing of power among levels of government. A union can use state-level lobbying to gain its ends when local-level negotiations fail. Twice in 1975, for example, the governor of Oregon intervened to avert a threatened strike by teachers. In both instances, he persuaded school boards to increase their offer and to break the stalemate.

Nevertheless, the Rand research suggests that end-run bargaining at the local level has produced very limited results for organized teachers. Seven of the fifteen districts in the fieldwork sample experienced one or more strikes. In all but two of these districts the mayor, city council members, or state legislators attempted to intervene and help resolve the impasses. But in no case did the third party effort facilitate settlement. Rather, the parties themselves or sometimes an outside professional mediator finally succeeded in ending the strike. Interestingly enough, both labor and management were critical of intervention by public officials, rarely requested it, and agreed that disputes were best settled by the parties directly involved. A recent study by the staff of the California legislature drew a similar conclusion in its assessment of California's newly implemented teacher collective bargaining law. Almost universally, involvement by elected officials was seen as counterproductive or of no benefit by both parties involved in the teacher collective bargaining law procedures.

Organized teachers seem to hold minimal expectations about the payoffs for their local-level electoral activity. Although fourteen of the fifteen teacher or-

---

⁴ F. J. Foley, "Public Employee Unionism in Pennsylvania: Impact on Local Power Distribution," (Paper delivered at the 71st Annual Meeting of the American Political Science Association, San Francisco, September 2–5, 1975), p. 37.

ganizations studied in-depth supported candidates for local school board offices, only two of them were found to wield much political power as a result of this activity. The rest viewed their support of political candidates as a defensive action. Because the position of school board member is usually both a thankless and nonpaying job, it is often difficult to encourage competent people to seek this office. Teacher organizations report that they support board candidates to reduce the risks of poor leadership. Organized teachers hope that if they contribute campaign funds and manpower, they might encourage better candidates to run. But once their candidates win, the teacher organizations seem not to expect the kind of payoff or access that they receive from the state and national candidates they support. Board members who had received such support concurred with the teachers' assessment. Consistently across school districts, members elected with teacher organization support attempted to remain independent even during collective bargaining.

In the study, interesting contrasts appeared between the two teacher organizations that had real political power. Both groups played critical roles in electing mayoral and school board candidates who were responsive to organized teachers, and both had managed to get a school superintendent discharged. Here the similarities ended. The first organization operated in one of the poorest urban school systems in the country. The problems of poverty, low student achievement, and general deterioration confronting this district existed before the rise of the teacher organization. Yet the organization failed to use its extraordinary control over school district policy to improve the system. Rather, it successfully deflected the district's efforts at reform; it used its veto power over school policy to maintain the status quo in both district and school-site policies.

The second organization, on the other hand, was a progressive political force within the city and school district. Organized teachers acted effectively to minimize opposition to school desegregation and to bring about peaceful compliance. Operating in a state without a public employee collective bargaining law and in an environment hostile to organized labor, the organization required political influence at the local level to survive as a collective bargaining agent. Consequently, it worked to elect a proteacher school board. But the organization used the power that it obtained constructively. Both labor and management felt the relationship was a productive one. Most potentially controversial issues were settled through the use of joint labor-management committees operating at both the district and school levels. Finally, although the teacher organization placed its own self-interest foremost, it used its power to improve conditions for students. For example, it succeeded in having a provision included in its contract guaranteeing that all students be given vision and hearing tests.

Since the fieldwork sample was chosen as a representative of a larger, random sample, it is fair to assume that the conclusions reached about local-level political activity are valid for other districts in the country. Most teacher organizations support local candidates, but few receive much payoff for such support, and few expect any. Only a minority of local organizations have attained appreciable political power; a few of these have abused it, while others have found a way to pursue their own self-interests and still work to improve the quality of educational services delivered to students.

Political activity by organized teachers at the state level is a different story. In many capitals the state affiliates of the two national teacher organizations are among the most powerful lobbies. NEA state affiliates receive the bulk of teacher membership dues and use the funds for professional lobbying as well as for substantial research and public information programs.

Teacher organizations typically pursue three goals. The first is to obtain greater financial support for public education. In pursuing this objective, the teacher organizations ally themselves with other educational interest groups, including administrator and school board associations.

Second, they work for the enactment of public employee collective bargaining laws or toward the improvement of existing laws. Teacher organizations have been joined in this endeavor by other public employee groups and private sector organized labor. Twenty-nine states now require collective bargaining between school districts and organized teachers. In other states the teacher organizations strive to elect candidates who will favor such legislation. A teacher organization, in a state that narrowly defeated a public employee collective bargaining law, recently joined with other unions to oust an incumbent legislator who refused to vote for collective bargaining legislation. This effort involved thousands of dollars in campaign contributions and many hours of donated manpower. Many felt that the labor groups were demonstrating their power to other legislators who wavered in their support of collective bargaining legislation.

Third, organized teachers pursue by means of state statutes the kinds of gains typically associated with local bargaining. Included here are minimum salary schedules, maximum class size, and requirements for the employment of school specialists. This pursuit constitutes a classic bypass or end-run around local districts. Attaining such provisions through state legislation ensures an inflation in the base on which local bargaining proceeds. Needless to say, these legislatively secured mandates compromise the flexibility of local school management. In one state, for example, compliance with 1978–79 statewide salary minimums will require raises for two-thirds of all teachers.

State school boards associations generally lack the means to counteract teacher influence at the state level. Often a single large urban district will wield more power in the state capital than the school boards association. In many states the school boards association remains weak and amateurish. They lack the financial resources and, more important, the manpower needed to support political candidates. The few school board members are simply no match for large groups of organized teachers, who can walk precincts and operate phone banks.

State level political activity by organized teachers is unlikely to diminish over time. Indeed, it will probably increase. Educational policymaking has become more centralized. Many decisions, traditionally the sole prerogative of local school boards, are now being decided at the state and federal levels. For example, recent judicial rulings requiring the equalization of school finance mean less local control over taxation and spending policies. Organized teachers have both responded and contributed to this centralization, and now that it has accelerated they realize that there are limits on collective bargaining gains at the local level. Consequently, teacher organizations are concentrating more of their energies on state-level political action.

The recent movement for tax and public expenditure limitations, evidenced by the passage of Proposition 13 in California, also carries profound implications for the collective bargaining process. To the extent that other states respond like California, which assumed more of the cost of public education, local collective bargaining could diminish in importance. State control of the purse strings could cause the emergence of a two-tier system of bargaining in which most of the negotiating occurs at the state level. Bargaining on items that have no direct cost implications, such as teacher evaluation, transfer policy, and student discipline, could remain at the local level. But such a radical transformation of the collective bargaining system still seems at least several years away. It also seems clear, however, that teacher organizations will increasingly look to the state to meet demands formerly made on local school boards.

The shift toward state lobbying and political action stems also from a growing disenchantment with such militant tactics as strikes. Strikes have proven to be counterproductive. Not only have public attitudes turned against striking teachers, but school boards are now better equipped to deal with teacher strikes. Many school districts have formed mutual aid pacts that allow administrators from nonstriking districts to assist a strike-bound district in keeping its schools open. In addition, the oversupply of teachers usually means readily available substitutes. The following scenario is more and more common: teachers strike; schools remain open; the district receives its per pupil support from the state; the wage bill for lower-paid substitutes falls; and the district derives financial profit from the strike. The only real losers are the striking teachers who often must settle for the district's prestrike offer or even less in some cases.

"Teacher power," then, involves both the contractual gains made by organized teachers and the results of their state-level political action. But, as teacher organizations focus on state and federal political action in the hope of gaining control over aspects of collective bargaining and school finance, the responsibilities and autonomy of local school boards are simultaneously weakened.

Implications for Local School Governance

Using a dual strategy of collective bargaining and political action, organized teachers have won contractual gains at the local level and secured political gains from higher levels of government. Although these gains are not total or universal, local teachers have acquired a number of noneconomic items in their contracts that may greatly limit the flexibility of school management. Smaller class size and more teacher preparation periods mean more money in the personnel budget and less for discretionary programs. Strong involuntary transfer provisions constrain district efforts to meet faculty desegregation mandates. Reduction-in-force provisions based on seniority not only interfere with the retention of younger and sometimes more competent teachers but also raise the salary costs. State-level legislation that regulates class size, sets minimum teacher salaries, and establishes teacher evaluation procedures will further reduce the latitude of local school boards.

The growing influence of organized teachers raises questions central to educational governance: To what extent do the interests of organized teachers differ from those of other actors in the educational policy arena? Will the delivery of educational services improve or worsen because organized teachers have a greater voice in the process?

No definitive judgment on the educational effect of growing teacher power is possible. On the one hand, organized teachers have demonstrated a preference for certain types of innovative programs and opposition to others. Teacher organizations support programs whose effect is to reduce student-teacher ratios, employ more educational specialists, and generally increase the number of teachers employed in the public school system. Teachers also want educational policies that reinforce the authority of professional educators and give them control over program implementation. Both the NEA and the AFT strongly oppose voucher plans that create a market system in elementary and secondary education. Such schemes threaten the job security of public school teachers and make them more accountable to local, nonprofessional community and parent groups. As suggested by a slogan often repeated by teacher groups, "Teachers Want What Children Need," organized teachers feel best qualified to evaluate priorities in public education. In keeping with this philosophy, teacher organizations have resisted attempts to impose accountability criteria devised by outside agencies and have continued to emphasize seniority as the basis for retention and promotion.

When they evaluate alternative educational policies, organized teachers sort out their various interests, among which the acquisition of basic skills by students is only one. Self-interest is always present and at times may conflict with what other groups define as the best interests of students. However, to argue that the self-interest of teacher organizations affects the delivery of educational services is not necessarily to say that the classroom learning process is adversely affected.

In fact, the evidence suggests that greater participation by teachers in district- and school-level decisions may facilitate implementation of innovative programs and hence work to improve classroom instruction. Recent research on federally funded innovative programs found that teacher morale and willingness to expend extra effort were important determinants of program success.[5] A

---

[5] Paul Berman and Milbrey W. McLaughlin, *Federal Programs Supporting Educational Change,* 4 (Santa Monica: Rand Corp., 1975), p. 20.

similar study that focused on reading achievement concluded, "In general, the more active was the role of teachers in implementing the reading program, the more reading achievement improved."[6] To the extent that teachers enjoy autonomy in their classrooms and a voice in structuring the learning process, they can positively affect the quality of instruction.

Teacher collective bargaining has produced mixed results. Organized teachers have undoubtedly constrained local school management in some important ways. But bargaining emerged as the solution to decades of low salaries and arbitrary treatment by school administrators. Collective bargaining has provided teachers with more autonomy in their daily work life and promises to make them full-fledged participants in the educational policy process.

The nation needs to ensure that teachers do not become the preeminent voice in education to the exclusion of parents, school administrators, and the general public. A balanced interplay among these interests can best be maintained at the local level, where professional lobbying staffs, public relations programs, and other expensive capabilities can be kept to a minimum.

Inevitably, decisions about how to finance the schools will move to higher levels of government. But this does not obviate the role of school boards in critical questions of curriculum content and the delivery of educational service. State legislators must leave such areas of decision-making for local action. Indeed, most legislatures appear to have little interest in replacing local school boards as the dominant governing body in public education.

At the local level, school management must realize that although the future gains of organized teachers are unlikely to equal those made in the late 1960s and early 1970s, teacher collective bargaining is not going to disappear. When the process works well for both sides, all interests gain. The Rand research found that collective bargaining functions most satisfactorily if three conditions exist: first, a mature and well-established bargaining relationship with accepted negotiating and grievance procedures; second, respect between the leaders of the school district and teacher organizations who, though they disagree, perform their respective jobs in a professional manner; and, third, a good working relationship betwen the parties that permits regular informal consultation and features incentives for both sides to settle disputes as quickly as possible.

In summary, teacher collective bargaining has profoundly altered patterns of local school governance. Boards of education and school administrators have less management flexibility than in the past. But fears about the preeminence of teacher organizations at the local level seem unfounded. Rather, as collective bargaining relationships mature, compromises will emerge and in most districts organized teachers will continue as one among a multitude of competing interests.

---

[6] David Armor et al., *Analysis of the School Preferred Reading Program in Selected Los Angeles Minority Schools* (Santa Monica: Rand Corp., 1976), p.52.

The State Role in Regulating
Local Schools

MICHAEL W. KIRST

Although many countries have established nationally regulated public school systems, the United States has always emphasized local control of education—leaving most questions of what and how children are taught to the discretion of 16,000 local districts. During the last two decades, however, policy-setting power in American public education has become increasingly centralized, and this shift of authority over academic policy is cause for alarm.

There has been an explosion in the number of regulations affecting schools. For example, state and federal courts, which in the past had little to do with shaping school programs, today set detailed priorities about issues ranging from student rights to bilingual education. Meanwhile, on the federal level, Congress provides funds for everything from schools in low-income areas to education for the handicapped—but, inevitably, with strings attached.

Recently the balance of power has shifted away from the local level and toward the state level. Federal revenue sharing and conversion of federal categorical money to state block grants are giving states more influence. At the same time, states are limiting the policy prerogatives of local governments through school finance reform, accountability, and other means of regulation.

One of every four Americans is now enrolled in institutions offering formal instruction. With over 3 million employees of schools and other educational agencies, education consumes the largest percentage of most state budgets (e.g., 70 percent of Florida's unearmarked revenues). Thus it is easy to see that too much is involved in schools for state politicians to leave educational issues to local authorities. Seats on the state legislative education committees rank only below those of appropriations and revenue committees in terms of status and desirability. Indeed, the number of pieces of state education legislation submitted and enacted has increased annually in almost every state. In California, the legislature passes an average of two hundred bills a year that affect local schools and add to the already bloated four volume State Education Code. The discretion of local officials in school policymaking shrinks as state education codes and regulations grow.

Under the Constitution, education is a power reserved to the states. The basis for state control over education was well established as early as 1820 by constitutional and statutory provisions. Most state constitutions contain language that charges the legislature with the responsibility for establishing and maintaining a system of free public schools. The operation of most schools is delegated by the state to local school boards.

Historically, the states have controlled local education through several means. The state may, for example, establish minimums below which local school operations cannot fall. The rationale behind such regulations is that the state's general welfare requires a basic educational opportunity for all children, and thus pupils may be required to attend school a minimum number of days each year or their instruction must include certain courses, taught in certain ways, with teachers who have a particular kind of training. In order to conduct this minimum program, the state may require school districts to levy a minimum tax and guarantee a certain level of expenditure, known as the foundation level of expenditure. This requirement of the state was originally intended to raise standards in rural schools. It also frequently included teacher credentials, building standards, and sometimes limits on class size.

States may encourage local schools to exceed minimums and often share some of the costs if local districts provide higher salaries or extend the school year. Some states allow communities to levy higher levels of local property taxes beyond those required to support the foundation level of expenditure.

Other states have specified or encouraged reorganization of school districts. For example, around 1900, states abolished the decentralized ward-based school boards in cities (Philadelphia had forty-three) and required a single citywide board and superintendent. In the 1940s, states began to require consolidation of school districts and eliminated so many that where there were nine school districts in 1932, only one existed in 1978. The total number decreased from 128,000 to 16,000.

States have required the provision of services, such as education for the handicapped. Indeed, a major argument for state control is that it can ensure equality and standardization of instruction and resources. Local control advocates, however, assert that local flexibility is desirable because the technology of education is so unclear. In essence, the argument over local control focuses on the trade-off between two values—equal (and adequate) treatment and freedom of choice. Moreover, the influence of laymen is more likely to be enhanced by the availability of local discretion for decentralized governance units like school boards. State centralists argue, however, that state minimums do not restrict local discretion. Over time, such requirements are transformed into a low level of school services, which is exceeded substantially by districts either with greater wealth in taxable property or with a greater willingness to levy taxes, or both.

States have tried to bring about greater efficiency in local education through devices such as requiring program budgets or standards for graduation. The local control advocates assert that educators in general and states in particular lack the knowledge to specify the most efficient educational methods. Consequently, local options are more desirable.

In sum, equality, efficiency, and choice are three values that often compete. The first two have been growing in public acceptance, and the state role has increased. Local options, on the other hand, have been curtailed.

Variations in State Control

States differ markedly with respect to historical patterns of control over objects of governance such as curriculum, personnel administration, and finances, depending on whether the state follows a "centrist" or a "localist" policy. In New England the local schools enjoy an autonomy from state controls that may have its roots in the hatred of the English governor, but textbooks and courses of instruction in the southern states are often centrally determined.

State curriculum mandating has both historical and political causes. Often newer subjects, such as vocational education and driver training, have needed state laws in order to gain a secure place in the curriculum. These subjects were introduced into the curriculum after 1920 amid great controversy, whereas mathematics and English never required political power to justify their existence. Consequently, the standard subjects are less frequently mandated by state laws.

Lying behind the interstate variation in local control is a concept called "political culture," which refers to the differing value structures that manifest themselves in the characteristic behavior and actions of states and regions.[1] Political culture ranges widely in its objects—political rules, party structures, government structures and processes, citizens' roles, and attitudes about all these. In short, political culture is a constraint helping to account for major differences among states in local versus state control. It affects policy feasibility. It also helps to determine whether state control will expand and the inclinations of local officials to evade state influence.

Frederick Wirt has conducted an empirical analysis of the variety and extent of state control in thirty-six selected areas of school policy and assembled statutes, constitutions, and court opinions for each policy.[2] He then constructed a scale of state control: absence of state authority, 0; permissive local autonomy, 1; required local autonomy, 2; extensive local option under state-mandated requirement, 3; limited local option under state-mandated requirement, 4; no local option under state-mandated requirement, 5; and total state assumption, 6. As table 1 indicates, the states display a striking diversity, from Hawaii's total state assumption of schooling, stemming from its royal tradition, to rural Wyoming. On the other hand, there is a concentration between 3 and 4 on the

---

[1] See Samuel C. Patterson, "The Political Cultures of the American States," *The Journal of Politics* 30 (February 1968): 187–209.

[2] See Frederick Wirt, "School Policy Culture and State Centralization" in *Yearbook on the Politics of Education*, ed. Jay Scribner (Chicago: University of Chicago Press, 1977), pp. 164–87. See also Wirt, "What State Laws Say About Local Control," *Phi Delta Kappan* 59 (April 1978), pp. 517–20.

centralization scale. Regional patterns are not clear-cut, but there is high local control in some states of the Northeast and high state control in some southeastern states. States clustering at each end are both rich and poor in economic terms. Size in terms of population or total square miles appears unrelated to scores on the scale. The "average state" of 3.56 has extensive state guidelines with some to few local options. However, the variety of state control is more noteworthy than the statistical average.

Wirt analyzed which areas of policy were characterized by the greatest state control. Table 2 presents the policies where there was the most state control. The "reforms" of earlier eras are clearly highlighted—personnel, compulsory attendance, records, and accreditation. Vocational education reflects the political organization and impact of the relevant interest groups at the state level.

Table 3 presents areas of high state control. Some of these policies represent the traditional state gate-keeping role (teacher employment, calendar, records, and revenue controls). Curriculum, student progress, and physical facility regulation are other major areas of high state control. Table 4 presents areas of moderate state control. Finally, table 5 reflects areas of nearly even divisions between states emphasizing extensive local control versus those stressing great state regulation. Included in this category are new programs, enrichment, pupil-teacher ratios, and evaluation; and it is in these areas that local authorities and citizens can have the most impact. These are not minor responsibilities, but they are being eroded incrementally in some states. Indeed, these

TABLE 1

School Centralization Scores and Ranks by States, 1972

State	Score	Rank	State	Score	Rank	State	Score	Rank
Ala.	4.67	3	La.	3.19	37	Ohio	3.65	22
Alaska	3.38	31	Maine	3.09	41	Okla.	4.91	2
Ariz.	2.91	43	Md.	3.56	27	Oreg.	4.30	6
Ark.	3.57	26	Mass.	2.73	48	Pa.	3.75	21
Calif.	3.65	22	Mich.	3.85	15	R.I.	3.21	36
Colo.	3.79	19	Minn.	4.10	8	S.C.	4.61	4
Conn.	2.68	49	Miss.	3.93	10	S.D.	3.08	42
Del.	3.15	39	Mo.	2.84	46	Tenn.	3.48	28
Fla.	4.19	7	Mont.	3.47	29	Tex.	2.88	45
Ga.	3.24	35	Nebr.	3.81	16	Utah	3.42	30
Hawaii	6.00	1	Nev.	2.84	46	Vt.	3.17	38
Idaho	3.26	34	N.H.	3.13	40	Va.	3.88	13
Ill.	3.32	33	N.J.	3.87	14	Wash.	4.37	5
Ind.	3.90	11	N.M.	3.79	19	W. Va.	3.94	9
Iowa	3.80	17	N.Y.	3.63	24	Wis.	3.62	25
Kans.	3.38	31	N.C.	3.80	17	Wyo.	1.86	50
Ky.	3.90	11	N.D.	2.89	44			

Source for tables 1–5: Frederick M. Wirt, "What State Laws Say about Local Control," *Phi Delta Kappan* 59 (April 1978): 517–20. Reprinted with permission.

TABLE 2
Policies of Highest State Control

Policy	50-State Score	Number of States with Total Assumption
Certification	5.50	33
Vocational education	4.89	15
Attendance	4.64	12
Accreditation	4.50	27
Financial records	4.27	16
Median score	4.64	

TABLE 3
Policies of High State Control

Policy	50-State Score
Special education	5.09
Curriculum	4.41
Safety-health	4.37
Textbooks	4.35
Transportation	4.34
Teacher employment	4.17
Calendar	4.09
Graduation	4.06
Admissions	3.82
Construction	3.76
Records	3.71
Adult education	3.63
Revenue	3.57
Median score	4.09

TABLE 4
Policies of Moderate State Control

Policies	50-State Score
LEA organization	3.58
Library	3.51
Counseling	3.51
Educational objectives	3.41
Grading standards	3.38
Physical plant	3.36
Equal education opportunities	3.34
Salaries	3.30
LEA size	3.11
Median score	3.38

TABLE 5

Policies of Bimodal Control Patterns

Policies	50-State Score	Number of States with Requirements	
		Absent	High (5–6)
State accounting	3.14	21	27
Evaluation	2.99	22	23
Teacher/pupil ratios	2.69	22	21
Extracurricular activities	2.50	14	11
Expenditures	2.45	27	20
Experimental programs	2.24	25	15
Personnel training	2.09	24	12
Median score	*2.50*		

tables demonstrate how the state domain of minimum specifications has expanded while local discretion has contracted as compared to the nineteenth century.

Little is known about the operational impact of state mandates. It is known that state enforcement is sporadic and reacts to local complaints. There is no systematic inspection system. A survey of local perceptions and behavior is particularly needed to answer the following questions: Is practice consistent with policy, i.e., are state statutes and regulations enforced fully and effectively? What inducements or sanctions are most effectively employed in enforcement? Are distinctive patterns of state control in intergovernmental relations associated with distinctive differences in school outcomes or what the system delivers to children, i.e., do these differences in control make a difference in children's learning or in the availability of important inputs or processes?

Some of the major areas that signify the dramatic increase of state control within the last two decades are state administration of federal categorical grants, state role in education finance, state requirements for educational accountability, state specifications and programs for children with special needs, and state efforts to stimulate experimentation and innovation. The writer takes no position on the desirability of these state initiatives. The purpose of this essay is to assess their impact on local control.

These substantive changes were made possible in large part by an increased state institutional capacity for intervention in local affairs. Most state legislatures have added staff and research capacity, and they also now meet annually or for longer periods of time. State legislators are thus provided enough resources to formulate and oversee educational policy. Governors now have their own education specialists and improved fiscal staffs.

The capacity of state education agencies (SEAs) to intercede in local school policy has also increased dramatically in the last twenty years. Ironically, the federal government provided the initial programmatic and fiscal impetus for this expansion. The Elementary and Secondary Education Act of 1965 and its subsequent amendments required state agencies to approve local projects for federal funds in diverse areas such as education for the disadvantaged, handicapped, bilingual, and migrant children, and innovation. In each of these federal programs, 1 percent of the funds were earmarked for state administration. Moreover, Title V of ESEA provided general support for state administrative resources, with some priority given to state planning and evaluation. By 1972, three-fourths of the SEA staffs had been in their jobs for less than three years. All the expansion in California from 1964 to 1970 was financed by federal funds. In 1972, 70 percent of the funding for this agency in Texas came from federal aid. The new staff capacity was available for SEA administrators or state boards that wanted a more activist role in local education.

Local control advocates such as teacher unions, school boards, and administrator associations feud among themselves and provide a vacuum that state control activists can exploit. These education groups cannot agree on common policies with their old allies such as parent organizations, the American Association of University Women, and the League of Women Voters. The loss of public confidence in professional educators and the decline of achievement scores have created an attitude among many legislators that local school employees can no longer be given much discretion.

State Accountability Mandates

Between 1966 and 1976, thirty-five states passed accountability statutes, and fourteen claim to have "comprehensive systems" with several components. Despite a lack of common definition and concepts, 4,000 pieces of accountability literature were published. In effect, accountability has focused state control on school outcomes in addition to state-defined minimum inputs. Some of the areas where state accountability control has expanded are requirements for new budget formats (including program budgeting), new teacher evaluation requirements, new state tests and assessment devices that reorient local curricula to the state tests, state mandated procedures for local educational objective setting, parent advisory councils for school sites, and state specified minimum competency standards for high school graduation.

In Florida, for example, these various accountability techniques interact to enhance state control. State assessment tests in certain subjects are publicized through parent councils. Statewide tests are also required for high school graduation. Students must score in the seventieth percentile statewide to obtain a diploma. Student test scores are related to teacher evaluations. School districts fear the adverse publicity than can come with publication of test scores lower than other districts.

Recent court cases, including *Serrano* v. *Priest*, and political movements have given impetus to increased state financing of education. The major policy thrust has been to enhance equality in per pupil expenditures. About twenty states that include 60 percent of the pupils in the nation have revised their finance laws, increasing state aid and sometimes decreasing local options to levy property taxes or to raise expenditures. While control does not necessarily follow the dollar, in some states it has. In California, state policy has attempted to reduce the discretion of local education agencies to spend money and restrict their ability to increase expenditures each year. Low-spending districts, however, have more flexibility because they are receiving more state aid and can increase their spending up to the state average. State legislators are often unwilling to expand state aid without attaching strings and accountability requirements.

The newest state finance reform is related to the tax limitation movement. If such a limitation focuses on the local property tax, as it did in California's Proposition 13, then local choice will be eroded. The California property tax is limited to 1 percent of the assessed valuation, and there is no way local voters can increase their school expenditures beyond that level. An unintended effect of Proposition 13 was state control of all education finance and the elimination of the ability to raise funds locally for construction of schools by selling bonds. Therefore, given the California tradition of extensive intervention, state control will increase. For example, after Proposition 13 passed, the state required local school districts to give priority to child care and adult education. Many local boards wanted to reduce these two areas significantly.

It is possible that state finance reform and movements like Proposition 13 will stimulate statewide teacher bargaining. If the state controls all funding increases, then teachers must negotiate with the state for salary raises. Consequently, a two-tier approach may develop. Some issues such as salary schedules and fringe benefits would be bargained for at the state level, and other areas of school policy would be reserved for local negotiations. Two tiers, however, would restrict the ability to reach compromise solutions because trade-offs between economic salary issues and other considerations, such as teacher preparation periods, would not be possible.

The right to strike is an equally difficult area in statewide bargaining. In the event of a statewide strike, could the governor stand the pressure to get children back to school and also give priority to the future impact of increased state costs? Probably most legislatures would find the strike issue untenable and choose binding arbitration. A related issue is the supposed negative impact such bargaining would have on educational experimentation. Statewide negotiated agreements would tend to be uniform. Regional bargaining might provide more flexibility, but regional boundaries are exceedingly difficult to devise.

The demand for equal opportunity has spawned new state programs for populations with special needs. States now classify children in several ways and mandate services and standards for the various categories of students. Some of these pupil classifications are vocational education, career education, the mentally gifted, the disadvantaged, migrants, underachievers, non-English speaking, American Indians, pregnant minors, foster children, delinquent children, and twenty or more different categories of handicapped children. Massachusetts, a state noted for its strong belief in local control, has adopted a sweeping special education law. It mandates entirely new education programs. New individualized evaluation procedures must be established and parents involved. New working relationships are required for teachers, psychologists, and other specialists. New evaluation techniques are outlined to avoid misclassification.

State bilingual education programs imply similar requirements. In California, any class with ten or more pupils whose English is limited must have a state specified program. Federal programs for the disadvantaged and handicapped require the states to impose additional requirements on local school approaches to populations with special needs. The states must determine if the local proposal meets federal regulations. Several states have started their own programs for the disadvantaged that build on the federal concept. In short, states have been suspicious of local initiative and commitment to disadvantaged and minority populations without state regulations.

State government has also been skeptical of local willingness to adopt innovative programs. Consequently, states have started innovative categorical programs for which localities must compete. Massachusetts has an experimental school program that combines magnet schools for multiracial populations with community control. California has the School Improvement Program, which provides over $100 per pupil to school-based councils composed of parents, teachers, administrators, and high school students. These school site councils are charged to devise new ways to individualize education and meet other state goals.

Some of the state innovation programs provide greater local flexibility. Legislation permits noncertificated people, including lawyers, craftsmen, and artists, to teach courses. In addition, some states permit waivers of requirements if the local district can provide a special justification for such a waiver.

Is State Control Too Much?

While much of the federal, court, and state legal and bureaucratic entanglement in local education comes from a legitimate need to correct past failings, such as the neglect of minorities in public schools, the pendulum has swung too far. This is especially true in states with high control ratings on the Wirt index. Moreover, there is no counterforce to this growth in centralized control. Dominant political and social forces are all moving in the same direction toward ever more court, federal, and state intervention in local policymaking.[3] For example, there is no national or state leadership pushing for a complete reorganization and pruning of state education codes that would eliminate traditional regulations requiring substantial amounts of money. State mandated collective bargaining was not accompanied by repeal of some personnel restrictions in existing state codes. States continue to set standards for personnel and pupil-teacher ratios based on an era when teachers were not permitted to bargain. This is not the kind of emotional issue that provides political dividends.

[3] See Tyl Van Geel, *Authority to Control the School Program* (Lexington: D.C. Heath, 1976).

Education has received poor publicity in recent years for a variety of reasons —declining enrollments and test scores, vandalism, lack of discipline, and soaring costs. This provides a rationale for state officials to continue intervention in order to reform local education. Moreover, many state officials believe local school districts will neglect the needs of disadvantaged, bilingual, and handicapped children. States have increased their aid for specific purposes because they believe local boards are not tough enough to resist teacher demands for exorbitant salary increases. Increasingly, local officials cannot act unilaterally but must take state regulations or guidelines into account before they act. In many instances, state officials must be consulted to see if the regulations can be interpreted to permit a specific local initiative.

At this critical juncture, new structures for school governance are needed to restore faith in local control and reverse the erosion of local prerogatives without slowing progress toward equal educational opportunity for all children. A new definition of local control is needed to focus on discretion at the level of the individual school as contrasted to the traditional approach of local school boards as the key to change. The primary role of federal and state governments should be to provide resources and stimulation for major decisions and changes in the schools. A first step toward achieving this goal would be a reorientation of priorities from the turn-of-the-century reforms of centralization, depoliticization, expertise, and civil service competence. The new priorities would be increased lay control, representation, the school as the unit of governance, and decentralization—including a reversal of the trend toward state control.

How would school site decision-making work specifically? There is no one best system, and various localities need to use different forms. One version would work as follows. A prerequisite step would be a complete overhaul and pruning of the state education code to permit more local options. Then each school would elect a citizen-staff council composed of parents, teachers, administrators, and perhaps high school students. Large amounts of state and local unrestricted funds would be allocated to each school to spend as it chose. Newport-Mesa, California, has a small-scale version of this system. It results in markedly different funding patterns; some schools stress more books, others more counselors. The school council would decide the instructional priorities (how much time for basics) and school organization (open or traditional classrooms). At the end of a three-to-five year contract, the council would recommend the retention or replacement of the principal to the central authorities. Collective bargaining with teachers would be at the district level (wages, for example), but some issues (curriculum or choice of textbooks) would be reserved for the school site council. As in San Jose, California, at each school the teachers may want to form a faculty senate that would elect representatives to the school site council and discuss other major site issues. This would help overcome the isolation of teachers that has impeded cooperative school planning. Education policies cannot be imposed on unwilling teachers. Certainly, if individual school decision-making is viewed as a device to undermine teachers' rights and collective bargaining, it will surely fail.

Now there is a profusion of overlapping and uncoordinated parent advisory groups at each school as mandated by federal or state law. Most of these groups could be eliminated. For the remainder, the citizen members of each individual school council could meet separately and approve applications for federal and state categorical aid. An annual report of school performance would be sent to each home, including information on program expenditures, educational processes, pupils' test data, and other outcomes such as pupils' self-concept and vandalism.

The central school district has a crucial support role for staff and parents' training, evaluation, and oversight. The role of the central district would probably be more extensive for high schools because of such needs as work-study and off-campus programs that can best be coordinated centrally. Experience in some states, such as Florida, demonstrates that school site decision-making requires preparation for principals, teachers, and parents.

This type of governance plan embodies the recognition that the individual school, rather than the entire district, is the critical nexus between the child and the substance of education. The individual school is also large enough to have relevance for state aid formulas. Is money for special federal and state programs reaching the schools with the greatest number of needy pupils? It is important to know, moreover, whether such schools are receiving an equitable share of the local district's budget for "regular" programs. Even in school districts with three or more schools, it is the local school site that is the primary concern of many parents. Even where community participation is not great at all schools, this plan would have beneficial effects, since the issue of how things are done and how people feel about their governance is crucial.

One must question the reformer's assumption that the community is an entity for the purposes of educational policy and that, consequently, there should be a uniform educational program in all schools. Within one school district in Florida the percentage of students in elementary schools who did poorly on tests ranged from 22 percent in one school to 78 percent in another. It is clear that this diversity in skills requires diversity in practices, programs, and instructional methods of schools. With safeguards to prevent racial and economic segregation, the emphasis on the school site can be linked to the concept of varying program clusters selected by parents. Schools in the same geographical area could feature different approaches—open classrooms, self-contained classrooms, and schools without walls—and parents could choose the one they deemed appropriate for their child. All alternatives could be within the public sector to avoid the difficulties of an unregulated voucher scheme. A plan with such choices would provide parents greater leverage over school policy. Schools that experienced declining enrollment would lose part of their funding.

This new focus on the individual school would be accompanied by a strengthening of the central school board. The school board would continue to make broad policy decisions regarding such issues as desegregation, while educators at each school site, guided by the views of parents, would have greater control over that school's budget, staff, and curriculum. The central school board could enhance its effectiveness through hiring its own independent staff analysts rather than relying solely on the superintendent's staff. In large local education agencies, school board members should receive salaries that enable them to surrender part of their nonschool activities. In sum, if the governance structure at the local level is revitalized, a stronger justification for returning to local control of education policy is possible. Without such rethinking, the present centralizing trend is destined to continue.

Alternatives for
Future Federal Programs

JOEL S. BERKE
ELIZABETH J. DEMAREST

Intergovernmental program administration is the principal mode by which the goals of the federal government are expressed and implemented in American education. This essay will discuss some current problems and potential changes in American educational federalism. It will identify issues in contemporary programmatic strategies, administrative mechanisms, and intergovernmental roles, relate these issues to emerging trends, and suggest alternatives for the future. It will emphasize programs designed to further equality of opportunity, the principal priority of federal education efforts in recent years. Although this discussion will be limited to elementary and secondary education, the argument is applicable to a broader range of federal activities in education.

The 1960s demonstrated that the federal government could enter novel and volatile educational areas, enact dozens of new programs, increase its appropriations fivefold, and become an influence in virtually every school district in the land. As the federal emphasis in the 1960s shifted from earlier noncontroversial activities like school milk and lunch programs and vocational education aid to the enforcement and facilitation of desegregation and the support of education for children in poverty, an adversary relationship often came to characterize intergovernmental relations in education. Whereas previous federal aid laws had been accompanied by rather innocuous pro forma state plan requirements, the legislation of the 1960s was implemented through a series of detailed regulations, guidelines, and program memorandums intended to ensure compliance by presumably unenthusiastic or hostile state and local education agencies. Whereas most previous federal legislation was seen as helping state and local education agencies accomplish their own objectives, the new programs of the 1960s were widely perceived as serving federal objectives with state and local education agencies merely a convenient administrative apparatus.[1] In a decade of rapidly growing school populations and rising educational costs, however, the growing financial assistance from Washington was accepted as a blessing, although a mixed one.

The 1970s have illustrated how permanent this enlarged federal role has become. Despite opposition by two Republican presidents committed to restraining federal activity in domestic policy areas, expansion continued to occur in both the number and the size of federal education programs. In higher education, the goal of equal educational opportunity led to vast new programs of student aid. In elementary and secondary education, new target groups were singled out for assistance: children with limited English speaking ability, the handicapped, and migrants, among others. As a proportion of total revenues for public elementary and secondary education, federal aid remained where it had stabilized in the late 1960s, at a little less than 8 percent. Because it was concentrated in carefully defined categorical areas, however, its impact on state and local practice often proved more significant than dollar outlays would suggest. Furthermore, some states and local districts began to demonstrate a commitment to similar goals by creating categorical programs that paralleled the federal ones.

While the reality of federal participation and influence was firmly established, administrative tensions continued to grow. State and local dissatisfaction with reporting requirements and program restrictions increased apace, and the Nixon-Ford administration efforts to consolidate individual programs into block grants received considerable support among state and local school people. But representatives of the groups that benefited from existing categorical programs prevailed. The block grant approach, successful in achieving general revenue sharing and in other areas such as housing and urban development, made only the slightest dent in the system of carefully compartmentalized categorical aids for education. For Democratic authorizing committees in Congress, sharply specified categoricals were the principal mechanism by which they could pursue their education policy interests in the face of a hostile White House. The development of regulations and guidelines within the federal education bureaucracy reflected little of the Republican administration's professed zeal for dismantling the infrastructure of federal influence.

In the first two years of the Carter administration, no radical changes were made in the direction or structure of federal education activities. The Education Amendments of 1978 retained the basic elementary and secondary categorical structures and programs, even creating ten new small programs of aid. The most notable substantive revisions were new sections of Title I of the Elementary and Secondary Education Act of 1965 (ESEA) to provide more funds to central city and poor rural districts and to encourage states to enact or expand their own compensatory programs. In the administrative aspects of the law,

[1] Michael W. Kirst, "Federal Aid to Education: Who Governs?", *Federal Aid to Education: Who Benefits? Who Governs?*, ed. Joel S. Berke and Michael W. Kirst (Lexington, Mass.: D.C. Heath, 1972).

there was some movement in the direction of easing paperwork requirements and turning over more responsibility to the states for monitoring and enforcement. In terms of education directions, the emphasis on equality of educational opportunity remains paramount, but the amendments include some modest new concern with encouraging states to emphasize basic skills education, to conduct statewide testing programs, and to ensure that private schools participate more fully in federal programs.

The role of Congress appears to have changed surprisingly little with the transition to a chief executive of the majority party. Executive-congressional discussions in developing the elementary and secondary legislation in 1977 and 1978 were conducted at arms length, and while the administration got much of the modest change it sought, its attempts at substantial reform in impact aid and in the creation of a new quality education initiative were substantially rebuffed.

While HEW and the education committees of Congress were concerned with rewriting the elementary and secondary aid laws, the President's Reorganization Project and the Senate Committee on Governmental Affairs were actively engaged in what is the chief education initiative of the Carter administration, the creation of a cabinet level Department of Education. The argument for the new department was presented with little consideration—even some administration denials—that the proposed organizational changes might have implications for the substance and direction of the federal government's activities in education. The hearings in Congress turned largely on which components would be included and what the internal administrative structure would be. By the time the bill passed the Senate and the House completed committee action, all agencies with any political clout had escaped being combined with the existing Education Division. On internal structure the Senate and House bills diverged; the Senate provided detailed organizational specifications, and the House reflected the administration's desire to provide flexibility for the first secretary of education. In the final, hectic days before adjournment for the 1978 elections, the bill failed to reach the House floor.

In the Ninety-sixth Congress the administration will renew its efforts to achieve a cabinet post for education. If the initiative succeeds, one of the first orders of business for the first secretary of education will be to take stock, to assess the potpourri of educational goals, programmatic strategies, and intergovernmental roles that he or she will inherit, with an eye toward developing recommendations for greater coherence and effectiveness in the future.

An Inventory of Intergovernmental Issues

An examination of intergovernmental aid mechanisms reveals that federal categorical programs in elementary and secondary education vary greatly. Program goals include advancing equal educational opportunity, improving linkages between education and work, encouraging innovation, and providing limited general assistance. Some programs use a "service support" approach that provides services for groups or purposes neglected by other levels of government; others are "capacity building" programs that develop local resources to meet new needs; still others are research, development, or demonstration programs. Intergovernmental arrangements for administering these different types of programs differ. Compounding this complexity, closely related federal equal opportunity objectives are pursued through enforcement of civil rights guarantees, as well as by categorical aid.

Despite differences in goals, approaches, and administrative arrangements, most federal programs use similar strategies designed to ensure that the funds are used for the purposes intended. With few exceptions, they are targeted for particular categories of aid and may not be used for general purposes. They are supposed to supplement local resources rather than replace them. These grants also attempt to exert leverage on the distribution of state and local resources or to bring change in traditional educational approaches. Finally, most programs specify a process that must be followed in operating and developing such programs.

Federal categorical programs may focus their efforts on specific groups (disadvantaged or handicapped children or those with limited English language skills), particular services (libraries or teacher training), or certain subject areas (vocational, science, or metric education). As equal educational opportunity has gained in priority, the target group focus has gained in relative importance over other types of categories.

Categorical education grants tend to be structured and operated as if program target groups were separate and identifiable. While it may be relatively simple to distinguish any one of these groups from the general school population, as the number of categories has grown it has also become necessary to distinguish special need populations from one another. This task is complicated by the existence of an as yet undetermined amount of overlap among the groups. It is unknown exactly how many children with limited English language skills are also educationally disadvantaged (i.e., perform below grade level), but a high correlation is obvious. Similarly, many children in the "soft" handicappped categories (i.e., learning disabled, emotionally disturbed, and speech impaired) could easily be considered educationally disadvantaged and qualify for services if they live in eligible attendance areas.

In addition to creating areas of overlap, the present system of categories also leaves gaps in services. Some children who could profit from special services often occupy these gaps. No comprehensive picture of the nature and extent of such gaps is available, but anecdotes can suggest some. For example, certain categories of mildly handicapped children in non-Title I schools may go unserved. If states define their handicapped population to include these children, they must serve all of them with their own funds. However, if state service mandates do not cover these children, those in Title I schools may be eligible for federally financed Title I services. Also, until recently, children who moved out of Title I schools in connection with desegregation plans or for other purposes lost services. This gap has been partially filled by amendments to the Emergency School Aid Act of 1972 (ESAA), which permit use of those funds to "follow the child" with compensatory programs when the move is in connection with desegregation, but loss of services from types of mobility not covered under this amendment may still occur.

The overlap and gaps in federal target group populations suggest a number of policy and service delivery issues. From the national policy perspective, it may imply adjustments in existing estimates of the size of individual special need populations as well as the aggregate number of special need children. These phenomena also have budget implications. The difference between "full funding" of existing authorizations and current appropriations levels may be less than is now believed if multiple eligibility and overlapping were factored out. Accurate estimates of where the gaps are would vary from state to state, depending on the inputs made by parallel state or local district programs.

At the point where services are actually delivered to the child, target group overlap and gaps pose dilemmas in deciding which children should be served. Local districts may opt to coordinate programs and provide each child with one service to the extent that funds are available, but in so doing they may run afoul of various funds allocation requirements in the individual programs that are intended to protect their supplementary nature. Alternatively, districts could allocate all their services independently. This could lead to a "stacking" effect where some special need children would receive two or more services while other eligible children receive none. Given the propensity in some districts to play it safe and avoid audit exceptions, a third scenario is possible. Districts may hold up services to some children while officials negotiate with state education agencies or the U. S. Office of Education (OE) to obtain clarification on who should be served with which revenue source.

The notion that federal money supplements state and local education expenditures is basic to the structure of federal categorical assistance. The original idea was that the state and local levels would continue their normal expenditures for the basic school program and the federal money would go on top of that base to be used exclusively for special services tailored to the needs of national priority groups.

Most federal education legislation contains allocation requirements intended to prevent state and local governments from using federal funds to replace their own. Almost all federal programs include statements that federal funds must "supplement and not supplant" state and local money. A few programs further stipulate that federal funds may be spent only for the excess costs of the special programs. In following these requirements, federal program officials tend to view intergovernmental funding patterns as a series of layers. First, local funds must finance the basic program. Next, state funds are to be applied without regard to the availability of federal aid. Finally, federal assistance makes up the top layer, with occasional disputes among federal officials as to how money relates among their own programs.

Research suggests, however, that this concept is not typically followed at the local level. More often, local administrators engage in what David Porter has called "multipocketed budgeting."[2] That is, they plan their programs and review all their income sources, including federal aid, to find the needed resources. Funds are symbolically allocated to accounts that satisfy federal requirements, while in reality local priorities are pursued. As the total number of income sources proliferate, the restrictions imposed by a particular source become increasingly less meaningful because tracking the use of funds is more difficult.

Another factor that has made the layering concept increasingly difficult to implement is the blurring of the early distinction between the supplemental sphere in which the federal government operated and the basic education sphere in which the state and local governments operated. This has occurred as more and more states voluntarily create their own supplemental programs or provide supplementary services in response to civil rights mandates. Although program regulations attempt to provide guidance in the gray areas, a recent National Institute of Education (NIE) study identified the "supplement not supplant" provision in Title I as one of the most complex and least understood requirements in that program. When a rule acquires an abundance of qualifications, it may be time to reevaluate the rule.

All categorical grants aim to influence what state and local school districts do. If this were not the case, the federal government would provide only general aid. Leverage may be sought indirectly. One goal of Title I of ESEA and other programs, for example, is to focus attention on groups that have been neglected in the hope that this emphasis might spur a rethinking of priorities at other levels.

Federal grants also employ two types of more direct leverage—matching requirements, through which other levels of government pay a share of the program costs, and funds allocation requirements, which affect the level or distribution of state and local spending or seek to place controls on other categorical programs. Matching requirements have not been utilized as much in education as they have been in some other social service areas. The vocational, adult, and handicapped education programs contain matching requirements, but the basic Title I of ESEA and bilingual education grants do not, except for the small, new incentive program to match state compensatory education programs.

The extent to which funds allocation requirements are utilized by programs to obtain leverage over state and local funds also varies. Vocational education would be on the weaker end of this spectrum and Title I at the stronger end. Almost all programs contain "maintenance of effort" requirements that prohibit reductions in state and local spending below previously established levels. Title I also includes a requirement for comparability that requires roughly equal state and local expenditures in Title I and non-Title I schools. The general purpose of requirements of this type is further to protect the supplementary nature of the grants by preventing "supplanting," the replacement of local dollars with federal dollars.

[2] David O. Porter, *The Politics of Budgeting Federal Aid: Resource Mobilization by Local School Districts* (Beverly Hills: Sage Publications, 1973).

Title I is also an example of a program that contains requirements that seek to influence how other categorical monies are spent. Program regulations require that Title I children be "equitably provided" with state and local funds—that is, such children must get the same share of state and local categorical funds as they would have received without Title I. Another provision prohibits the use of Title I funds to provide services required by state law, court order, or various civil rights guarantees. Given target group overlap, the effect of these requirements is to move additional funds to the Title I constituency. If relatively high amounts of funds are available or if funds are applied in an uncoordinated way, these requirements could result in the stacking effect mentioned earlier in which some disadvantaged children (in Title I schools) receive multiple services while other disadvantaged children (not in Title I schools) receive none.

Most federal education legislation relies in theory on the local level for program development. The General Education Provisions Act (GEPA), for example, contains a specific prohibition against federal control of educational curricula and programs. Such provisions are a reaction against traditional fears of federal control, a recognition of the claim that educational decisions are best made at the local level, and a result of the fact that federal programs often attack a problem without a clear understanding of the proper solution. In fact, however, the federal government exerts a good deal of direct influence over programming supported with its own funds and indirect influence over the wider system. This effect occurs in several ways.

Some federal education legislation specifies a process that grantees must use to develop their programs. Again, Title I is a good example. It requires a needs assessment, quantifiable objectives, concentration of resources on a limited number of children, program evaluation, and parent advisory committees. The process is an indirect attempt to encourage better compensatory education. Other programs, such as handicapped education or migrant education, place the locus of program development responsibility at the state level and require that a state plan be developed describing how the program will be conducted.

Still another type of program control is the direct or indirect mandate in some programs for particular educational methods or approaches. The handicapped program requires placing children in regular classes. Title VII of ESEA encourages bilingual-bicultural education over other methods of dealing with limited English language skills. Title I has, in the past, informally encouraged pull out programs and presently encourages programs to focus on basic skills.

In addition to issues of vertical relationships in intergovernmental aid, the existence of a multitude of federal categorical programs also raises issues of horizontal coordination at the federal, state, and local levels. As noted earlier, many states have created their own categorical programs paralleling federal efforts. For example, sixteen states spend a total of $364 million for compensatory education programs and twenty states and territories provide $68 million for bilingual education.

Little attention is given to coordination among programs in Washington. Interest in problems spanning the education system as a whole tends to be pushed aside by the pressures of day-to-day business, as policymakers deal only super-ficially with long-range trade-offs and cross-cutting issues. Farther down the organizational chart, in the middle levels of the bureaucracy, organizational, political, and budgetary incentives favor fragmentation. OE is set up along pro-gram lines. Separate bureaus or divisions generally focus on different target groups. Interest groups are narrowly focused. The classic triangle of bureau, interest groups, and congressional committee supporters, whose main interest is protection of "their" children, has grown up around each program. Also, since none of the programs is fully funded and all want to expand, tight budget con-straints create incentives for competition rather than cooperation.

States vary greatly in their style of implementing categorical programs and in their attitudes toward coordination. A number of state agencies have shown considerable leadership in trying to coordinate the myriad federal programs with one another and with their own state categoricals. One recent study described grants coordination techniques used in fourteen states, largely at their own initiative, such as standardized applications, consolidated planning, and consolidated programs. The study found that, while these innovations had led to some administrative improvements, their success was disappointing. The varied federal requirements were contradictory, federal officials were perceived as being nonsupportive of state efforts to coordinate, and bureaucratic rivalries often developed at the state level among the separate program offices.[3]

Local districts, depending on their size, may have from fifteen to one hundred sources of funding. Since they actually deliver services, they must somehow fit all the pieces together. Local officials appear the most likely to complain about "unnecessary restrictions." Yet there are indications that local officials are often reluctant to deal creatively with coordination problems, because they are uncer-tain about what is required by federal law or regulation and they fear federal audit exceptions. Recent congressional hearings found persistent instances of federal programs that were poorly coordinated with one another and federal and state programs that were not coordinated, even at the school level.

Federal influence on state and local education agencies is also exerted through civil rights guarantees. The federal government has pursued the two basic strategies of compliance and technical assistance.

Since 1967, federal civil rights enforcement activities to promote educational access have been centralized in the HEW Office for Civil Rights (OCR). OCR is responsible for ensuring compliance with various statutes, executive orders, and court decisions prohibiting discrimination based on race, national origin, sex, or handicaps. OCR identifies possible violations through systematic review of racial enrollment data to locate gross imbalances that may signal violations, through response to individual complaints alleging violations, and through regular compliance reviews. If these indicators suggest problems, school districts may be selected for comprehensive on-site compliance reviews. Grantees found in violation may face termination of federal funding. With the

[3] Meredith A. Larson, *State Efforts to Reduce the Paperwork Burden of Categorical Education Programs* (Menlo Park, Calif.: SRI International, March 1978).

exception of ESAA, which requires civil rights clearance before awards are made, there is no formal coordination between OCR civil rights enforcement and OE program activities, even though they are focused on the same target groups and share the general goal of promoting equal educational opportunity.

Responsibility for technical assistance related to civil rights, which is intended to encourage voluntary compliance, is split between the OE Office of Equal Educational Opportunity Programs and OCR. The former handles technical assistance under Title IV of the Civil Rights Act covering race, sex, and national origin, while OCR handles section 504 technical assistance covering handicaps.

The groups covered by civil rights guarantees, with the exception of the educationally disadvantaged, tend to parallel the groups benefiting from categorical assistance programs. This suggests a potential for reinforcement, but little effort has been made so far to coordinate these levers. Although the bulk of the enforcement burden is on OCR, most studies find OCR's performance highly inadequate. The traditional rationale is lack of staff; however, some recent studies have suggested other explanations. A study examining the relationship between civil rights and program directives in selected areas found a number of conflicts in goals and strategies. Another study of Title IX enforcement suggested that lack of clear policy goals and direction from the HEW leadership is the main stumbling block to improved enforcement.[4] Clear and complementary goals are a precondition for effective coordination for related program and civil rights mandates.

In sum, federal intervention in education is based on premises and strategies that developed incrementally over time. These may have been well suited to a smaller and simpler system but appear increasingly inappropriate as the system continues to evolve toward greater complexity. Among the most significant developments that existing federal assumptions fail to reflect fully are program proliferation and the associated problems of overlap and gaps, the growth of a parallel but uncoordinated systems of categorical aid and civil rights mandates, and the maturation and increased sophistication of state agencies and local districts.

Establishing an Effective Intergovernmental Partnership

The intergovernmental partnership in education has heretofore been honored more in rhetoric than in reality; federal strategies are still oriented toward control and are in many respects uncoordinated. Yet changes in state and local behavior toward special need categories, desired in the 1960s, have begun to take place. With growth of state categorical programs in compensatory and handicapped education, minimal competency initiatives, and civil rights guarantees, a rationale for federal involvement that rests on the idea of doing what other governments neglect is no longer fully accurate. Not all states have as yet made specific commitments to federal goals, but a policy that recognizes

---

[4] NOW Legal Defense and Education Fund, *Stalled at the Start: Government Action on Sex Bias in the Schools* (Washington, D.C.: PEER Project, NOW Legal Defense and Education Fund, 1977).

the accomplishments that have been made and provides incentives for more states to move in the desired direction seems preferable to one that reflects the environment as it was fifteen years ago. A philosophy of federal-state partnership, therefore, seems the most suitable for the 1980s.

Recent political history suggests the infeasibility of radically dismantling the existing structure of federal aid to education and replacing it with block grants. Substantive considerations suggest its undesirability as well, for the present categorical apparatus provides needed guarantees and protections for target groups that have long been the victims of discrimination or neglect. Reform proposals must address the problem of molding these helter skelter policies into a simpler and more coherent system, while maintaining those strings essential to accomplish federal objectives in the decentralized governance structure of American public education. This interpretation of contemporary issues and political constraints suggests a modest agenda for future changes in strategy, funding, and administration.

Emphasis on serving identified target groups has spawned a number of restrictive and competitive policies that often prove dysfunctional, fragmenting a child's education in order to preserve individual program audit trails. Strategy for the future should seek to provide greater flexibility without resulting in general aid. Reform should focus on easing restrictions that apply among target groups, while retaining distinctions between special need groups and the general school population. With new authority to shift funds among closely allied categorical areas, an important step would be taken toward three important objectives: reducing overlap and filling gaps among categories, lessening the complexity of compliance with federal law, and permitting coordinated attention to the educational needs of pupils.

Substantial revision is needed in the tangled web of fund allocation provisions. An area where more flexibility could be provided is in situations where state and federal programs seek basically the same objectives. State and local officials pursuing goals similar or complementary to those of federal aid programs ought to be able to use all the funds available to them in a mutually reinforcing manner.

As already discussed, however, funds allocation requirements designed to prevent supplanting or to leverage other federal, state, and local funds are complicated, tend to restrict the nature of the educational approaches used, and are inconsistent from program to program. The control afforded by these indirect fund allocation requirements is less necessary if resources are increased. Since significant increases in federal spending for education are unlikely in the near future, a policy of greater reliance on state matching requirements could be pursued. Replacing some indirect controls with matching requirements would implement the philosophy of partnership, permit program simplification, and make the relationships between state and federal policy objectives more visible and explicit.

Revision of federal funds allocation requirements is of particularly high priority at present because more than fifteen states during the last five years—some under court order—have undertaken to revise their financing systems to achieve greater fiscal equalization and greater focus on special education needs. While no comprehensive federal program yet exists to achieve the same fiscal objective sought by this movement for school finance reform, a number of separate legislative provisions have expressed federal approval and encouragement of such state efforts. However, except for section 5d(2) of the impact aid law, a provision designed to avoid a conflict between the intrastate distribution of impact aid funds and state efforts at equalization, little attention has been directed at harmonizing federal aid and state finance equity objectives.

Another area of needed change applies to process requirements. One necessary element of partnership is trust, and federal procedural requirements currently reflect little of it. Substitution of output or performance standards for process requirements would be consistent with the partnership philosophy. In developing the regulations that would permit states to avoid conflict between impact aid and state finance equalization programs, HEW established standards drawn from developments in school finance reform laws. HEW made no attempt to specify the type of finance provision to be employed by states but permitted all states that met the equity standards to qualify for more flexible use of Impact Aid within the state. Although significant conceptual and technical problems are involved, the development of such standards in other regulatory areas would serve to redirect attention from paper pushing exercises to the product to be delivered or the educational outcome to be achieved and would permit greater latitude for state discretion in designing the means to accomplish program goals. This approach would also permit differential treatment of the states, depending on the nature of their objectives, the level of their financial commitments, and the degree of their administrative effectiveness.

More controversy has been stirred by the federal efforts to ensure civil rights in education than by any other federal program goal. A more comprehensive approach to civil rights goals would require that guarantees and assistance programs be mutually reinforcing. For example, protections against discrimination on the basis of national origin contained in Title VI of the Civil Rights Act and assistance for bilingual education under Title VII of ESEA could be handled in tandem to achieve more effective results than either alone provides.

Second, it is important that civil rights standards make sense educationally. For example, there is an uneasy coexistence between requirements for serving only schools with concentrations of poverty children under Title I of ESEA and desegregation policies, which stress dispersing minority pupils. Similarly, districts that observe civil rights requirements in other respects violate OCR regulations if they seek to assign minority teachers or administrators to schools with high proportions of minority pupils in order to provide role models.

A concerted effort to relate civil rights and educational policies should be made. Underlying such policies must be more effective cooperation between OE program administrators and OCR enforcement officials. Clearly, each agency has different operating styles and priorities, but without better communication, coordination of basic assumptions and strategies, and joint planning activity, the overall goal of achieving effective equality of educational opportunity for minority children may not be served.

Conclusion

Underlying any attempt to reform elementary and secondary education should be a commitment to establishing a working partnership between the states and the federal government. An increasing number of states have come to share federal goals and have begun similar programs of their own. In such instances, restrictive federal strategies should be loosened. The capacity to shift funds among closely related target groups and to take account of related state and local sources of support should be made possible. Funds allocation provisions, which indirectly exert leverage over state and local resources, should be explicitly reviewed and revised in light of state level reforms to promote equity in school financing. Matching requirements should be relied on more often as an alternative to complicated funds allocation provisions in order to promote an explicit federal-state partnership in accomplishing educational objectives.

Procedural requirements also need revision. The goal, wherever feasible, should be for federal aid programs to set performance or output standards geared to differential state conditions and designed to give states significant discretion on the means used to meet the standards. Finally, the relationship between civil rights requirements and educational program goals should be more closely linked. Related assistance programs and enforcement activities can be more closely linked to accomplish more in tandem than either accomplishes in isolation.

Forming a working intergovernmental partnership to improve education will require these and other revisions in current operating procedures. They will also require some changes in attitudes. At the federal level, the carrot and stick mentality of dealing with adversaries should be replaced wherever possible by the development of shared objectives and activities. At the state and local levels, officials must recognize the legitimacy of the federal interest in the nation's education, grounded as it is in the constitutional powers to tax and spend for the general welfare, and to enact laws implicitly necessary to carry out the explicit powers of government.

Educational governance and finance in the 1980s will require the collaborative efforts of all levels of government. The reforms suggested above are a short set of examples of how such cooperative activities could be encouraged and improved.

Changing Patterns of School Finance

JOEL D. SHERMAN

The financing of elementary and secondary education has historically involved all three levels of government. The locus of funding, however, has shifted markedly. Until the first three decades of the twentieth century, public schools were financed almost exclusively from local revenues derived from the property tax. State governments provided less than 20 percent of all educational costs, and the federal government contributed less than 1 percent. One result of such a system was a great diversity in expenditures among school districts within the same state. Districts with large property tax bases could provide higher levels of expenditures and better, more extensive educational programs and services than districts with small property tax bases.

During the 1920s and 1930s, many states began to adopt school finance formulas designed to reduce these expenditure disparities. Under the equalization formulas enacted at that time, property-poor districts began to receive more state aid per pupil than districts with strong tax bases. As a result of these new statutes, the state share of educational costs increased significantly, and the local share showed a corresponding decline. By 1940 the state share had reached 30 percent, and by 1950 it averaged 40 percent nationwide.

After a period of relative stability between 1950 and the mid-1960s, the secular shift in funding of public education to higher governmental levels resumed with the passage of the Elementary and Secondary Education Act of 1965 (ESEA). The federal share of educational costs increased from 4 to 8 percent in a single year. Since the late 1960s, the state share has risen further—to approximately 47 percent—as state governments have again become concerned with the problems of unequal expenditures and taxpayer equity.

At the same time the financing of public education has been shifting to higher governmental levels, there has been a corresponding shift in the locus of decision-making authority away from local school officials. The growing number and scope of state and federal regulations, standards and restrictions, mandates imposed by state and federal court decisions, and restrictions imposed by collective bargaining agreements have all worked to circumscribe the power of local school boards so severely that their ability to shape educational policy has been seriously questioned. To both educational practitioners and scholars, the simultaneous occurrence of increased state and federal financing of education and decreased local autonomy suggests a relationship between the two phenomena that is frequently believed to be causal. The conventional wisdom is that increased funding of education from nonlocal sources inevitably leads to increased centralization of control over school policy.

An assessment of the impact of changes in the locus of financial support on educational decision-making is unfortunately complicated by several factors. First, the concept of local control is such a highly cherished political value, with its origins dating back at least two centuries, that any action infringing on it—either in theory or in practice—is viewed with suspicion or hostilitiy. The debate about the loss of local control, and the relationship between finance and control, is more often marked by rhetoric than by sound research. Second, there is relatively little empirical research on this issue. Only a few studies have been conducted, and these are somewhat flawed in their research design. States or other jurisdictions with different levels of financial support from central sources are compared on various measures of centralization of decision-making at a particular time. Little empirical research critically examines the relationship between finance and control in one state or in several states over time. It is therefore almost impossible to trace the impact of changes in finance on the locus of decision-making.

Despite the emotional nature of the debate about local control and the limitations of existing studies, the small body of literature does provide some insight into the relationship between finance and control and the impact of shifts in funding to higher governmental levels on the locus of control over educational policy. This essay will review the available evidence in an attempt to assess the implications of changing finance patterns on educational governance. First, however, an overview of major recent developments in school finance in the 1960s and 1970s is necessary.

Recent Developments in School Finance

With the passage of the Elementary and Secondary Education Act of 1965 (ESEA), the federal government undertook a large-scale commitment of resources to educationally disadvantaged children from low-income families and, in a two-year period, doubled its share of revenues for elementary and secondary education from 4 to 8 percent. Since the 1960s the federal share of public school support has stabilized at about 7 to 8 percent, although the federal commitment to special need populations has been expanded to include the handicapped and bilingual children. It is estimated that by the end of the decade the federal government will spend annually about $3 billion on Title I of ESEA, about $1 billion on the education of the handicapped, and about $500 million on bilingual education. In addition, the federal government has begun to provide financial assistance to help states develop aid systems that more completely equalize the ability of local school districts to finance education. However, these funds are quite modest and a major federal role in financing equalization is unlikely.

In contrast, the role of state governments in school finance has grown significantly during the 1970s. One impetus to new school finance legislation and to an increase in the state share of educational costs has been a series of court decisions that have ruled existing school finance structures unconstitutional. The opening wedge for school finance reform through judicial mandate was the 1971 ruling of the California Supreme Court in the landmark case of *Serrano* v. *Priest*. In that case the court held that a school finance system that makes the quality of a child's education a function of the wealth of his parents and neighbors violated the equal protection provisions of both the California and the United States constitutions. In 1973 the United States Supreme Court ruled in *San Antonio Independent School District* v. *Rodriguez* that wealth-based inequalities in expenditures did not violate the equal protection guarantees of the United States Constitution. After *Rodriguez*, potential school finance reformers could not pursue the issue in federal courts, but the state courts were still open to them. Law suits have been filed in several states and many courts. Courts in New York, New Jersey, and Connecticut have ruled school finance systems unconstitutional on the basis of state constitutional provisions.

Many state legislatures have enacted new school finance statutes, some of which were specifically intended to reduce or eliminate the effects of school district wealth on educational expenditures. A unique feature of some of the new formulas that distinguished them from traditional school finance formulas was the possibility of "recapture" of local revenues. Local districts with strong tax bases had to contribute a portion of their local property tax revenues to the state for redistribution to poorer school districts. A number of states—including Utah, Montana, Maine, and Wisconsin—enacted recapture clauses, although a statewide referendum in Maine and a court decision in Wisconsin later rescinded recapture in both states.

More recent court rulings in states other than California have required that states do more than eliminate wealth-based expenditure disparities. They have raised questions about all differences in expenditures other than those related to differences in student needs, as well as focusing more on educational outcomes and achievement rather than costs. A 1973 decision of the New Jersey Supreme Court, *Robinson* v. *Cahill*, and a 1977 decision by an Ohio trial court, *Cincinnati* v. *Walters*, required that legislatures in these states develop systems of school finance providing all children with a "thorough and efficient" education. A more recent trial court decision in New York, *Levittown* v. *Nyquist*, suggests that the school finance structure in that state will have to take into account the special educational and financial problems of New York's major urban areas. Some observers wonder whether future court rulings may require equal expenditures for comparable children.

One characteristic of school finance in the states during the 1970s has been the imposition of limits on permissible levels or growth in school tax rates or expenditures. While these statutory limits on taxing and spending are not new in

American public finance, the recent utilization of such controls has been some-what more widespread than in previous periods. Several factors seem respon-sible for this phenomenon, especially the increased resistance of local taxpayers to mounting property tax burdens. The property tax revolt has manifested itself in an increased rejection rate for local tax and bond referenda and most recently in the passage of statewide initiatives in California, Nevada, and Idaho. These limitations may augur a further shift in the cost of education to the state level and further constraints on the decision-making capability of local school officials.

In sum, the trends in school finance over the last decade have been strongly in the direction of centralizing finance at the state level. Largely as a result of court pressure, many states have begun to finance a larger share of educational costs and made greater effort to reduce expenditure disparities among school districts. Several states have also provided greater financial support for special need students in high-cost programs. Finally, state governments have imposed tax and expenditure limitations on local school districts. It must therefore be asked, Has increased state funding resulted in—and will further increases result in—more state control of educational policy? On the one hand, will recapture provisions and court mandates of expenditure equality reduce local discretion? On the other hand, will higher state funding result in increased local control, particularly for poor school districts that are severely constrained in their edu-cational decision-making because of the lack of fiscal capacity?

The Relationship Between Finance and Control

The conventional wisdom relative to public school finance has asserted that higher levels of central funding are associated with more centralized decision-making and that upward shifts in funding responsibility are inevitably accom-panied by shifts in the locus of control. Only two multijurisdiction studies have taken cross-sectional views of the relationship between the proportion of central government funding and the degree of central regulation of educational deci-sion-making, and longitudinal studies of the impact of funding changes on decision-making have been limited to a few case studies. The findings of these studies, however, tend to contradict the conventional wisdom. Instead, the studies suggest that higher funding levels need not necessarily be associated with more centralized decision-making and that a loss of local autonomy does not inevitably result from an increase in state funding.

One of the earlier cross-sectional analyses of the relationship between finance and control, conducted by the Urban Institute, examined state laws and regula-tions in several areas, including curriculum requirements, budgetary and taxing restrictions, federal programs, and personnel in ten states with varying levels of state funding.[1] While the study was limited because no efforts were made to measure the extent to which regulations were in fact implemented, the conclu-sions were quite clear. The study found little relationship between the percentage

---

[1] Betsy Levin et al., *Public School Finance: Present Disparities and Fiscal Alternatives* (Washing-ton, D.C.: The Urban Institute, 1972).

of state funding and the degree of state restrictiveness on the operation of local school boards. The study also found that state restrictiveness in certain areas was not necessarily matched in other areas. For example, where state control of budgetary decisions increased, state control in other areas may have been reduced. In short, there were no uniform patterns when states were compared on several dimensions of decision-making at a given time.

A more recent cross-national study of primary school finance arrangements in ten OECD countries by the Centre for Educational Research and Innovation took a more limited view of local autonomy.[2] It focused primarily on local discretion over the major conditions of employment of teachers—e.g., numbers to be employed, their qualifications, and level of compensation—although a general assessment was also made of the extent to which local authorities could determine their schools' curricula and mode of operation. The study, which examined the relationship between the proportion of revenues for primary education derived from nonlocal sources and the degree of central government regulation of each of the areas of decision-making cited above, again found no clearly defined patterns linking finance and control. In some countries with over 80 percent of nonlocal funds, there was relatively little local discretion over the conditions of employment of teachers, while local autonomy was more extensive in others. Conversely, in some countries with under 60 percent of nonlocal funds, there was a wide range in local discretion over teacher employment and general school and classroom operations. In some countries central government regulation was quite extensive and local autonomy was restricted, while in others central regulation of school structure, operations, and program content was more limited. On the basis of the cross-sectional analysis, the study concluded that no simple relationship existed between the proportion of nonlocal funding and the powers of local school authorities.

The study did find, however, a fairly strong association between the extent of local autonomy and the mode of transferring central funds to local authorities. The study distinguished three main types of intergovernmental transfer: block, general purpose grants; service-specific, noncategorical grants (e.g., education, housing, and roads); categorical grants for specific purposes (e.g., teacher salaries, school building construction, and educational programs for the disadvantaged). The study found, in general, that noncategorical funding tended to be associated with higher levels of local autonomy than categorical funding. However, it was impossible to determine whether categorical funds were monitored effectively enough to ensure their use in the program areas for which they were intended or whether central government regulations were implemented consistently among local authorities. In light of the experience in the United States that has demonstrated that categorical funds frequently do not reach targeted populations but instead are used as general aid, the restrictiveness of categorical funding on local autonomy should be viewed with some degree of caution.

[2] Harold J. Noah and Joel D. Sherman, *An Overview of School Finance Arrangements in Ten O.E.C.D. Countries* (Paris: Organization for Economic Cooperation and Development and Centre for Educational Research and Innovation, 1977).

These cross-sectional analyses are, of course, useful in providing some insights into the relationship between finance and governance at particular times. However, they say little about the effects of changes in patterns of finance over time. A few longitudinal studies suggest that an increase in state funding does not inevitably imply a loss of local autonomy. A recent study conducted by the Stanford Research Institute for the National Institute of Education examined the impact of finance changes on educational governance in four states—Kansas, California, Florida, and Michigan—and concluded that increased state funding did not, and need not, lead to increased central control. Individual case studies of finance changes in several states, including Hawaii, California, and Florida, support this finding.

In 1965, Hawaii adopted a school structure in which the state became a single school district with seven administratively decentralized districts; total fiscal power was vested in the state. However, an assessment of the impact of this change on governance suggested that there was little infringement on local autonomy. In fact, state centralization of fiscal authority seemed to be accompanied by a decentralization of authority on nonfiscal matters. The consensus among legislators, state education department officials, local administrators, staff, and parents was that enough flexibility under the centralized system existed to ensure that programs could be adapted to the needs of local communities.

Recent developments in Florida and California parallel the developments in Hawaii. In both states, the legislatures have undertaken an extensive commitment to equalize educational expenditures among school districts, in part through a significant increase in the state's share of educational costs. At the same time, efforts were made to decentralize decision-making substantially by eliminating state regulations that were unduly restrictive. The new legislation in Florida also provided for the creation of parent advisory councils at the individual school level to encourage increased parental involvement in the school budgetary process. Similarly, the recently passed school finance statute in California provides for the creation of school site councils (groups at individual schools) and permits schools to apply to the state for planning grants to develop programs for school improvement. It is too early to determine whether these new governance arrangements will result in greater decentralized decision-making, although an initial evaluation of the Florida advisory councils suggests that most have had little impact. At least in theory, centralization of finance and decentralization of control are not incompatible, based on the record in several states. It must be noted, however, that there are components of the reform in all three states that do limit local fiscal discretion, particularly in regard to the level of expenditures.

The evidence developed in studies of finance arrangements in jurisdictions outside the United States supports the findings in American states. The Canadian province of Ontario, for example, initiated a large-scale effort during the late 1960s to equalize tax capacity and educational expenditures among school districts through adoption of an equalizing formula that substantially increased the provincial share of elementary and secondary school costs. At the same time that the province moved toward more centralized funding, however, it also decentralized decision-making over aspects of school organization and programs that had traditionally been strictly controlled by the provincial government. These included decisions about textbooks, curriculum, transportation, provision of kindergartens, and supervision of instruction. An assessment of the impact of these changes suggests that centralization of finance and decentralization of decision-making worked in tandem to enhance local autonomy. Boards that had previously lacked the resources to make both financial and programmatic decisions were able to do so after the change, largely as a result of the increase in provincial funding.

On the other hand, in several states new school finance legislation has been accompanied by a range of regulations that severely circumscribe local discretion. The school finance statute passed by the Colorado legislature in 1973, which was designed to equalize the tax base of school districts, contained stringent constraints on increases in school district revenues. The Florida school finance act of 1973 and the South Carolina school finance act of 1977 both contained provisions requiring a certain proportion of funds received by school districts as a result of pupil weighting factors to be spent on the pupils who earned the weights. At the federal level, there has been similar regulation of the use of federal funds, particularly Title I of ESEA, to ensure that funds are not used as general aid but are actually spent on targeted students. The designation of state or federal funds for particular programs or students has clearly limited local options on the use of these funds.

The changing patterns of educational finance and decision-making over the last few years are indisputable. The locus of authority over educational policy has clearly shifted away from local school boards to state and federal governments—and to nongovernmental institutions such as labor unions—while the financing of education has become less of a primarily local responsibility. However, as the preceding discussion has suggested, the relationship between these two phenomena is a complex one; it is difficult to determine with any degree of certainty whether centralization of finance is associated with—no less a cause of—centralization of control over educational decision-making.

Some recent developments in school finance suggest that future shifts in the locus of finance to state and federal governments may be accompanied by greater restrictions on local fiscal autonomy or greater monitoring of local use of state and federal grants in aid. First, the adoption of new school finance statutes in many states during the 1970s was accompanied by tax or expenditure limitations that, if fully implemented, could severely restrict the power of local school districts to increase their educational expenditures. Second, some new statutes that provided additional funding for special needs students through a system of pupil weightings set limits to the number or proportion of students who could be classified in different categories in order to prevent school districts from "overclassifying" students in categories that drew larger amounts of state aid. In addition, some of these statutes also mandated that funds be spent on the special needs students who earned the additional state aid, since school districts had often used these funds as general aid. Other provisions of this type suggest that as states increase their share of school costs, they may also attempt to regulate the use of these funds more carefully.

The impact of these regulations on local control, however, cannot yet be assessed, since most of them have been in effect for only a short time and it is still unclear to what extent they will be enforced. The tax and expenditure limitations enacted in several states contained provisions for waivers of the limitations either through an administrative review process or referendum. Early experience with administrative review procedures suggests that school districts that request waivers frequently receive them. While restrictiveness of these limitations on fiscal autonomy may be less severe than had been expected, they do appear to constrain the rate of growth in school expenditures.

The debate about the relationship between finance and control over educational decision-making will clearly continue as the locus of funding of elementary and secondary schools shifts toward higher governmental levels. The argument that increased central funding inevitably leads to a decline in local autonomy will be supported by the evidence cited above in which new school finance statutes that provide for higher levels of state funding are linked to new regulations of local fiscal decisions. On the other hand, the argument that finance and control need not necessarily be related is supported by the limited body of empirical research on the issue. Furthermore, whatever the pattern has been in the past, it may change in the future as greater emphasis is placed on educational outcomes and equal expenditures. Reforms intended to achieve these goals are likely to restrict local options more than past ones. Therefore, despite the changes that have taken place in school finance during the 1970s, it is still uncertain whether the conventional wisdom that "he who pays the piper calls the tune" is true.

Equal Educational Opportunity and Federalism

BERYL A. RADIN

Few areas of educational policy have been as volatile and conflict-ridden as those concerned with equal educational opportunity. Since 1954, when the Supreme Court called for an end to separate but equal school systems in *Brown* v. *Board of Education,* conflict between federal, state, and local educational systems over this issue has been part of the policy landscape. For twenty-five years, attempts to eliminate segregation from America's schools and to reach the elusive goal of "equal educational opportunity" have been variously greeted with violence, mobs, demagoguery, avoidance, and—too infrequently—with compliance.

The social change demanded by federal requirements in this area required a series of role shifts among the intergovernmental actors in education. After the *Brown* decision in 1954, federal courts began articulating standards for state and local educational agencies. With the passage of the Civil Rights Act of 1964 and the Elementary and Secondary Education Act of 1965 (ESEA), federal agencies assumed a more active role, developing national standards aimed at changing the balance of power in educational decision-making. In subsequent years, a variety of federal activities continued to impinge on the traditional set of relationships in the education policy system—that is, local control of education protected by state education agencies.

A variety of federal activities have thus affected attempts by state and local school agencies to achieve equal educational opportunity. Some of them resulted from federal court decisions enforcing statutory or constitutional provisions. Others resulted from categorical aid programs enacted by Congress and administered by the Office of Education in the Department of Health, Education, and Welfare, which provide aid either directly to local districts or indirectly through state education authorities. Still others stemmed from policies and programs supported by federally funded research efforts.

Although these activities share the common goal of achieving equal educational opportunity, they do not share common strategies and methods. The policies that federal courts have articulated tend to concentrate on racial and ethnic integration of school systems. Some of the categorical programs, on the other hand, have focused on schools that have concentrations of students with special needs. Other categorical efforts support attempts to raise the general level of academic achievement within the entire school system.

The various federal initiatives, administered by a variety of governmental bodies operating independently, have frequently left local officials and citizens confused and uncertain about federal procedures and goals. Streams of federal funds and policies, flowing from Washington—sometimes through federal regional offices, sometimes through states—finally reach local school districts where the pieces must be fitted together. It is not unusual for a child to be eligible for four or five separate federal programs. The multiple sources of funds and policies might not constitute problems for school districts if they did not often contain conflicting federal directives and seem to the school districts to leave gaps between mandated programs.

This multiplicity of policies and problems currently constitutes the most complex and difficult set of issues for those concerned about equal educational opportunity and federalism. The cry for states' rights and local control of schools— arguments that surrounded the mid-1960s debate on school desegregation and federal aid to education—is still sometimes heard. But more frequently, state and local school officials, as well as parents and other advocates of equal educational opportunity, are critical of the inconsistencies and confusion that surround federal programs.

Five Federal Efforts

An examination of the impact of some federal efforts related to equal educational opportunity illustrates the dimensions of the problem. These efforts include the directives of federal courts, the policies of the HEW Office for Civil Rights, Title I of the Elementary and Secondary Education Act, Title VII of the Elementary and Secondary Education Act (bilingual and bicultural programs), and the Emergency School Aid Act of 1972 (ESAA).

Although these five sources of federal policies do not constitute the complete repertoire of the federal government's efforts to ensure equal educational opportunity for all children, these efforts dramatically demonstrate the current problems. Not included are special programs and policies for women and handicapped children. The five programs also illustrate the evolution of federal efforts from relatively simple court orders to a multiplicity of policy actors and issues.

1. *The directives of federal court orders.* During the decade between the 1954 *Brown* decision and the passage of the Civil Rights Act of 1964, those who wished to invoke federal action to ensure equal educational opportunity were limited to litigation in the federal courts. During that period, "equal educational opportunity" was defined as the end of separate but equal schools, and the drive for equality was focused on the assurance of new opportunities for black children.

Although the cast of bureaucratic and client actors broadened considerably after the passage of the Civil Rights Act of 1964, federal court action continued to be a major technique to provoke change. In many school districts in the country, equal educational opportunity (particularly desegregation of schools) did not occur until local school boards were challenged by local citizens in federal court. When these courts found that constitutional rights of children were being abridged, they required local boards to develop plans to remedy that situation.

As the years progressed, federal court action broadened in scope. The first court orders concerned school systems segregated by race. Subsequent orders focused on denials of opportunities for children based on their ethnic background. They also widened the net of coverage to include some aspects of de facto as well as de jure segregation. ("De jure segregation" is the term used to describe segregation supported officially by law; northern-style segregation, usually known as "de facto segregation," describes segregation not sanctioned by official state action.) The remedies demanded by courts also shifted during the years, moving from consolidating school districts to quotas, pairing, clustering, closing schools, redrawing attendance lines, busing, and sometimes to requiring specific educational activities. The implementation and enforcement of court orders have frequently forced federal judges to act as administrators, educators, and community relations specialists.

2. *HEW's Office for Civil Rights.* The Civil Rights Act of 1964 was the first congressional action to enfranchise citizens who had been excluded from full participation in American society. Perhaps no part of that omnibus piece of legislation was more sweeping than Title VI—a general prohibition against discrimination in grants, loans, or contracts by all federal agencies. It also directed each federal department or agency disbursing funds to establish rules for implementation. Furthermore, the act gave agencies the authority to cut off funds from recipients if they failed to comply with these rules.

The Office for Civil Rights (OCR) was created in 1966 as HEW's centralized civil rights agency. The office was initially charged with enforcing Title VI provision, and as subsequent legislation was enacted, OCR's authority was expanded to include discrimination on account of age, sex, and handicapped status, as well as race and national origin. Although its authorization includes all HEW programs, OCR has tended to concentrate on compliance with civil rights provisions in education and has monitored public school districts and nonpublic schools that participate in federally funded programs.

OCR's responsibilities include the collection of data on the status of students and teachers. School districts under court order, in litigation, or undertaking voluntary desegregation, as well as those with concentrations of minority children, are required to submit information more frequently than other districts. The information gathered describes courses offered, achievement test scores, budgets, employment, and classroom statistics.

In addition, the OCR responds to specific complaints of discrimination through investigations and determinations of appropriate corrective measures. It has two additional functions in the education area; it is charged with enforcing nondiscrimination provisions for national-origin minority children, and it assists the Office of Education in the selection and review of applications made by districts for funds under the Emergency School Aid Act.

3. *Title I of the Elementary and Secondary Education Act.* The passage of the Elementary and Secondary Education Act of 1965 was the first large scale effort of direct federal financial support for the nation's public schools. Title I of that act was directed toward the education of socially and economically disadvantaged children and was a national testimony of faith in education as a way of breaking the cycle of poverty. Title I appeared to accept as social reality that concentrations of disadvantaged children were frequently isolated by race and educationally deprived. Rather than providing incentives to break up these concentrations or to desegregate the students within them, Title I targeted aid on the concentrations.

Although federal rules define the formula for allocation of Title I funds and set parameters for expenditures, the program operates differently in every state, in 16,000 school districts, and in numerous classrooms. State and local governments determine the substantive content of the program, refining the general program objective of contributing to the cognitive, emotional, social, or physical development of participating students. Districts, however, are limited in their ability to use Title I funds to replace existing state or local funds; students participating in programs funded by Title I must receive services paid for by state or local money comparable to those that other children in the system receive. Districts determine which schools among eligible areas of high concentration and low income will receive its Title I programs; various methods are used to define low income status. The federal regulations require districts to establish parent advisory councils, made up of a majority of members who are parents of children included in the program.

The program, unlike the other federal activities, most closely conforms to the traditional, multilayered structure of educational decision-making. It is federally financed, state coordinated, and locally implemented. The state education agencies administer all Title I programs within the state and act as a liaison between the federal Office of Education and the local school districts. The state agency allocates federal funds to localities in accordance with the federal formula, approves Title I applications, and—depending on its orientation—may monitor local programs and provide technical assistance to the localities.

4. *Title VII of the Elementary and Secondary Education Act—bilingual and bicultural programs.* Although a number of federal funding sources provide support for bilingual and bicultural activities, Title VII of the Elementary and Secondary Education Act explicitly provides funds to be awarded on a competitive basis to school districts with concentrations of students with "limited English speaking ability." Originally enacted as a 1968 amendment to ESEA, the program provides supplemental funds for a variety of programs that school districts believe will meet the special needs of large numbers of limited English speaking students.

When applying for the funds, districts must establish eligibility by showing that the children served are of "non or limited English speaking ability," are between the ages of three to eighteen, and come from low income families. Although school districts are told that they should coordinate their applications with state agencies, the funding is a two-party transaction between the federal agency and the local district. State agencies play no direct role in the determination of funding priorities, although a number of states with concentrations of these children have their own bilingual education laws that provide funds and have their own set of requirements.

Two major controversies surround federal bilingual programs, one involving a debate between advocates of "transition" approaches and those who argue for "maintenance" efforts. Those who support transition maintain that bilingual programs supported by federal dollars should move non-English speaking children into English speaking classes. Those who argue for maintenance believe these children should receive an education in their own language.

The second controversy surrounding bilingual education involves the enforcement of the Civil Rights Act of 1964 as it applies to limited English speaking children. In 1974, the U.S. Supreme Court ruled in *Lau* v. *Nichols* that denying these children a meaningful education constituted a violation of Title VI of the Civil Rights Act of 1964. The Court prohibited a number of educational practices—including assignment to special education classrooms, denial of access to particular courses (especially college preparatory courses), and permanent assignments into ability groupings based solely on language ability—on the grounds that they foreclosed students from a meaningful education. Although the Office for Civil Rights has taken steps to implement the Supreme Court decision, the Office of Education has not done so. Thus compliance or noncompliance with the *Lau* ruling is not a part of the criteria used to determine which school districts receive Title VII bilingual funds.

5. *The Emergency School Aid Act (ESAA).* The ESAA was enacted in June 1972 to provide local school districts with funds to meet special needs created by desegregation efforts and to encourage voluntary efforts to minimize minority group isolation in schools. The program was a third generation effort in this area; it followed Title IV of the Civil Rights Act of 1964 (to provide technical assistance to desegregating school districts) and the Emergency School Assistance Program of 1970, which included a program similar to ESAA.

The new legislation reflected congressional sensitivity to the special problems facing school districts as a result of desegregation. Although it contains a proviso that districts engaging in voluntary desegregation are eligible for funds, the major concern is with districts under federal court order to desegregate. Funds are available to local school districts and to nonprofit organizations that have programs to support local school desegregation efforts.

ESAA funds are allocated on a competitive basis. They may be used for a wide variety of activities that the district defines as playing some role in assisting desegregation. These include community relations activities, training of personnel, and compensatory education efforts. Funds are not filtered through a state agency; similar to the bilingual programs, the funding process is a two-party transaction between the federal agency and the local district.

Before the Office of Education can award a grant under ESAA, the HEW Office for Civil Rights must verify that the district receiving funds is in compliance with the department's civil rights requirements. If the district is under court order, it must admit to OCR that it is guilty of discrimination and must then apply for a waiver. Other districts that OCR finds not in compliance must correct the deficiencies or otherwise be ineligible for funds. If the district is under court order, it may not use any of the ESAA funds for efforts that are mandated by the federal judge, such as busing of children.

Local Views of Federal Efforts

Federal activity in each of the program and policy areas discussed above implies a criticism of the operation of local school districts. None of these efforts would exist if Congress, the courts, or individual litigants did not allege that districts failed to provide equal educational opportunity for all children. Thus it is difficult to put criticism of the programs from local school districts in perspective, since much of it reflects objections to the change demanded by federal requirements. School districts, like individuals, do not relish having to admit their biases. Neither do some school districts welcome the responsibility and trouble involved in developing new bureaucratic relationships, particularly ones that may bypass their traditional linkages with state education agencies.

It is extremely difficult to differentiate between complaints from school districts that reflect resistance to any sort of change and those that are valid concerns about irrational inconsistent federal policies. Often it is impossible to differentiate between a recalcitrant school district that is found in noncompliance because it refuses to provide equal educational opportunity for its students and a school district that is trying to form a comprehensive local effort in good faith and is found in noncompliance because of some technicality.

Federal efforts involving equal educational opportunity are volatile. Moreover, this situation is exacerbated by other factors that produce conflicting federal directives. To a large extent, these conflicts result from systemic biases of the American political system—incremental decision-making, political shifts over time, and the complexities of federalism. However, some conflicts have occurred because federal policymakers are unable or unwilling to assess the impact of their policies on local schools, the point of implementation. It is not that federal officials have asked questions and answered them "incorrectly." Rather, it is that few policymakers have asked the questions at all.

The development of a "rational" package of federal activities related to equal educational opportunity is blocked by three realities of the federal education policy system. While these factors are not unique to education policy, they do create a set of separate and specific problems for state and local education agencies: an inability to define a consistent federal strategy or set of goals, the nature of federal bureaucratic operations, and an inability to devise consistently applied but flexible federal policies.

During the quarter century of federal activities in this area, there has been no agreement on a single strategy for change. Two distinct and often contradictory approaches underlie the federal activity: desegregation (breaking up concentrations of children, whether by court order or through federal funds) and compensation (providing additional resources for children in their existing school settings). Regulations and requirements are largely used as the vehicle to achieve desegregation, based on prohibitions of certain types of behavior. Compensatory efforts, on the other hand, tend to use the availability of funds as the vehicle to promote change, using the strategy of incentives to shift behavior patterns.

The two strategies reflect very different theories about the cause of educational inequality. Those who advocate the desegregation strategy assume that inequities stem from patterns of racial or ethnic separation. Thus change cannot occur without solutions that drastically change those patterns. Advocates of compensation, on the other hand, take a more existential perspective. While they might admit that past inequities have been rooted in patterns of segregation, they argue that policies for change must be devised for children in their current situations. Thus solutions are developed around current distribution patterns and emphasize compensation for past problems.

The tensions between the strategies is not simply an intellectual one. The conflict plays itself out in confusing ways. For example, school districts operate Title I programs in compliance with certain requirements involving concentrations of low income children. However, if a district is under court order, children who had participated in Title I programs before busing may no longer attend eligible schools after busing. The situation appears to be counterintuitive: disadvantaged children should not be deprived of additional educational services because of a desegregation requirement. In one school district where this situation occurred, an OCR official told a federal judge that Title I funds should follow a child to a new school. However, the judge was also informed by a Title I federal official that this practice was prohibited.

The tension between the desegregation and compensation strategies is further complicated by the mutiplicity of federal actors involved in the development of equal educational opportunity policies: the courts, Congress, and the executive branch. Policies have continued to be articulated by federal judges. Although the major legal issues have been decided by the Supreme Court, a variety of decisions and remedies are fashioned by lower level federal judges. Most of the court decisons are variations on the desegregation theme. Some judges, however, have handed down orders stipulating that a district provide explicit compensatory programs.

During the fifteen years of congressional action in this policy area, marked shifts have taken place in the membership and in the rules of both Houses. In addition, a number of members of both the House and the Senate have shifted positions on desegregation issues as their constituencies have been confronted with desegregation·demands. In the past, congressional action produced a mixed strategy, mandating compensatory programs in some areas and establishing desegregation requirements in others. Support is now stronger for compensatory programs than for desegregation. In addition, congressional action tends to create specific categories of programs, each with its own set of interest groups, bureaucratic supporters, and congressional backers. The categorical decision process tends to create a fragmented and uncoordinated set of programs, each with specific target groups and specific activities.

Executive branch activity in this policy area is also extremely fluid, reflecting partisan shifts in the White House as well as changes in leadership in HEW and OE. Congressional willingness to accept administrative discretion in this policy field has also changed over this fifteen year period. Executive level agencies have been pushed toward more explicit enunciation of policies and requirements. In addition, because equal educational opportunity efforts originated in court actions on desegregation, the agencies involved in enforcing desegregation have had a special problem coordinating court orders with bureaucratic action. Court decisions that are fashioned to meet the unique requirements of a special case are difficult to translate into administrative rules and procedures. Conversely, courts sometimes find themselves stymied when they are able to establish rights but unable to create resources to make them materialize.

All these attributes of the equal educational opportunity decision process—conflicting theories about the causes of problems, a multiplicity of actors, and changing definitions—make it quite unlikely that a consistent strategy or set of goals will emerge, neatly defining the federal policy thrust in this area.

As additional programs and policies have been added to the federal equal educational opportunity repertoire, new agencies, policies, and procedures have been developed to administer the efforts. Although separate policy streams eventually intersect at the local school district level, their possible interrelationships are poorly defined in Washington. There are no mechanisms to devise consistent policies and procedures or to serve as an early warning system for possible conflict among efforts.

In part this conflict has occurred because of the bureaucratic division between civil rights and educational activities in HEW. The Office for Civil Rights operates for the entire department, although historically its major activities have focused on education. The education efforts, on the other hand, are administered through the Office of Education and the Education Division of HEW. A school district may thus be receiving instructions from two distinctly separate parts of HEW that do not operate in concert.

The bureaucratic separation also reflects different roles that HEW is asked to play. OCR serves as a regulator—a naysayer. The education programs, on the other hand, are in the business of dispensing money. Thus a school district may be negotiating with one HEW agency that is threatening to withdraw funding while discussions are under way with another agency that has funds to disburse.

In one case, OCR and an education program do have an institutionalized relationship in decision-making. OCR must review each ESAA application before funds are granted. Although the Office of Education uses the same basic format in determining grants for bilingual education, a similar relationship has not been devised for OCR review of the Title VII bilingual program applications. As a result, it is possible for a school district to be told that it is out of compliance with OCR policies involving limited English speaking children while receiving funds from HEW as the result of a bilingual education program application.

The OE itself is not always consistent in its bureaucratic procedures. A school district sends an application for Title VII bilingual programs directly to Washington. Application for ESAA funds are sent to one of the ten federal regional offices (or, in special circumstances, to Washington). Title I applications go to the state education agency, which in turn sends the state package to the federal regional office. Each of the programs has different submission and review dates, application formats, and review procedures. Some of these differences are based on statutory requirements or on congressional intent. Others, however, simply reflect the quest for bureaucratic turf.

Current proposals for the creation of a separate Department of Education have the potential of minimizing the conflict between OCR and the education program agencies. A new Department of Education would include a self-contained Office for Civil Rights with responsibility solely for education. However, the inconsistencies and problems within the Office of Education would not necessarily be affected by the creation of a new department. Indeed, some issues are not receptive to structural reorganization, and many procedures would require congressional action before any change could occur. However, increased sensitivity to these issues—either in a new department or within the current organizational framework—could lead to the development of mechanisms to detect inconsistent policies and procedures.

As the federal role in education has increased, so also has the urge for straightforward and predictable federal policies. It is argued that the requirements imposed on state and local school districts must apply equally across the country. Historically, arguments for flexibility in applying federal policies that involve equal education opportunity exhibited regional bias—imposing requirements on the southern states and ignoring northern and western states. But perhaps more important, flexible policies were viewed as a subtle way of maintaining the status quo. In addition, lawyers involved in the policy process were offended by arguments for flexibility in the application of requirements, since they believed it violated equal treatment before the law.

As policies and programs have proliferated and become more specific, the rigid application of requirements sometimes takes on ludicrous proportions. Education policies must apply to 16,000 school districts that vary tremendously in their student populations, faculty characteristics, community needs, political cultures, and district resources. Program and policy requirements are written to apply to what federal officials believe to be the "typical" district affected by the program. Even when they have correctly defined the characteristics of "average" districts, the specifications do not always provide sufficient latitude to be sensibly applied across the country.

For example, current requirements for the ESAA program stipulate that a school district receiving ESAA funds must establish an advisory committee with a membership that is one-third black, one-third brown, and one-third white. This specification applies even if the demographic characteristics of a school district are quite different from such a distribution.

Current policies involving equal educational opportunity do not acknowledge that school districts in some states may be faced with state requirements that do not agree with federal requirements. In some cases, such as state bilingual education policies, the state-federal conflict occurs because of the establishment of different state and federal priorities for programs and children.

Lack of flexibility is also a problem for local citizens who advocate change. The amorphous concept of equal educational opportunity takes on real meaning when applied to a specialized, local context. Local realities determine the specific application and definition of the term. Because of rigid policy definitions and also because of procedural limitations, federal policies determined in Washington frequently do not provide local parents and community advocates of equal educational opportunity with a chance to define their own remedies and strategies. For example, although funds are available through ESAA to local nonprofit groups, the funding is not available during the early stages of the desegregation planning process, a time when community opinions are formed and when such groups might play their greatest role.

Future Directions

Conflict between federal policies involving equal educational opportunity and local priorities can be expected to continue indefinitely. It is possible that a conscientious administration and Congress may be able to address the most blatant problems that stem from the multiplicity of programs and requirements. But the tension between federal and local education priorities will remain as long as local education agencies do not appear to be providing equal educational opportunity for all children in public school systems.

As long as the basic causes of the tension remain, one can expect that court action will continue to be a major vehicle for change. Categorical programs are likely to remain the congressional response to specific existing interests, as well as new ones. If neither the compensatory nor the desegregation strategy can demonstrate evidence of success, the conflict between the strategies will show no sign of resolution. In short, the intergovernmental education policy arena will continue to be volatile and ridden with conflict.

A Case Study of
Federal Involvement
in Education

DONALD W. BURNES

During the last quarter-century, the locus of educational policy-making in America has shifted dramatically from the local level to the state and federal governments. Starting with the Supreme Court's *Brown* decision of 1954 and the Great Society social reform programs of the 1960s, the traditional roles in educational decision-making have been transformed.

The growth of the federal government's involvement in education over the last two decades has been nothing short of phenomenal, as indicated by the increase in federal funding. Support of elementary and secondary education grew by almost 1,000 percent, to $8 billion, between 1960 and 1975. The U.S. Office of Education (OE) administered a handful of educational programs in 1964. Now almost 140 different federal programs are run by the OE staff that numbers over two thousand.

As federal programs have proliferated, the involvement of the federal government in the governance of education has also increased. Most of these federal programs have been designed to address specific needs of certain target groups of the educational population, either students or institutions (aid for such specific purposes is known as "categorical" aid, as opposed to "general" aid, which the recipients can use as they see fit). As a result, the federal government has found it necessary to do more than allocate funds in order to meet these needs; by establishing both rules governing the use of the federal dollars and mechanisms for monitoring and enforcing compliance with those rules, it has also given direction to local school districts as to the use of the money.

Local school districts have not always found the federal direction consistent with their own educational priorities. This has given rise to a fundamental tension about who should have the final word in determining how federal funds are to be spent in providing educational services for children. Should federal support be in the form of general aid, thus providing local districts greater autonomy and discretion in the use of funds? Or should the funds be categorical aid with more federal direction about the use of funds in pursuit of national priorities? If so, how extensive and specific should the direction be? These questions have been heatedly debated for a number of years, especially since the advent of large amounts of federal funding in 1965.

One of the programs that has played an important role in defining the extent of federal involvement in educational governance is Title I of the Elementary and Secondary Education Act of 1965 (ESEA). One of the first large-scale federal categorical programs, it is also the largest single program administered by OE. In fiscal year 1977 alone, Title I provided over $2 billion in funds for over 5 million students. Funding since the program began twelve years ago has totaled over $16 billion, providing programs for over 45 million children.

Although Title I provides aid for local school districts, it is not a simple grant-in-aid program for local jurisdictions. Title I funds are not for general aid; rather, they must be used to provide educational services in addition to those regularly provided to educationally disadvantaged students living in low-income areas. In an effort to ensure that the intended recipients receive special services, the federal government has developed an extensive management system for Title I. Through this administrative apparatus, federal officials provide direction to states and districts about who should receive Title I services, how these services are to be delivered, and under what circumstances.

This essay will examine the major parts of the Title I management system as a case study of federal involvement in education. Through this assessment, the essay will identify the strengths and weaknesses of the system and describe its impact on states and local school districts. It will also use evidence about the effects of the management effort to shed light on the more general issue of the desirability of this kind of federal involvement in education.

The Title I management system that has evolved since 1965 is the most extensive and fully developed of any that exist for the administration of OE programs. This system consists of four basic administrative functions: rule-making, dissemination, monitoring, and enforcement. In its rule-making function, the federal government has constructed a legal framework consisting of the legislation, as amended, the formal regulations and guidelines developed by the Department of Health, Education, and Welfare (HEW), and interpretive statements issued by OE to clarify the statute, the regulations, and the guidelines. The legal framework provides guidance to school districts about the use of Title I funds, the use of state and local funds in conjunction with these funds, and the ways in which services for students should be developed and delivered. The framework also contains requirements about state administration of the program and provisions relating to federal management.

The federal government disseminates the rules it has developed through several mechanisms. The more formal rules are published in the Federal Register and systematically distributed to all states and Title I districts. Less formal interpretive statements are disseminated in written form, typically on an individual basis in response to questions, or orally through national or regional workshops, or as part of routine site visits.

HEW also provides direction to states and local districts through its monitoring and enforcement activities. The OE program office, the Division of Education for the Disadvantaged, monitors performance through its annual program reviews of states and a small number of districts. In addition, the HEW Audit Agency conducts formal audits of a limited number of states and local districts to verify that states are performing their administrative responsibilities and that local programs are being managed as intended.

The enforcement function is carried out through the application of sanctions. OE can reject a state's annual application for funding, if it determines that the state is not administering the program appropriately. When auditors find that a state or district is out of compliance with the rules, OE can also penalize the jurisdiction by requiring the return of misspent funds.

During the first several years of the program, the federal management system, as it then existed, proved to be almost totally ineffective in ensuring that congressional intent was being met. The rules that existed did not adequately address the various types of problems confronting states and districts. Internal monitoring of activities was virtually nonexistent, and little effort was made to apply sanctions when audits did uncover abuses. As a result, several studies indicated widespread misuse of funds, and typical program expenditures flagrantly violated various legal provisions, especially those prohibiting general use of funds.

However, as the federal system has developed in the last several years, it has become more effective in ensuring that Title I funds are used as intended. The legal framework has been expanded to protect against certain types of abuses. More extensive mechanisms for program monitoring have also been established, thus allowing greater review of the performance of state and local districts. Consequently, "Title I administration is probably better now than at any time since the program was enacted."[1] In contrast to the early years of the program, Title I funds are not being used as general aid. Districts are increasingly providing special services to Title I children to supplement those that the students would normally receive. States and districts are meeting the wishes of Congress in their use of Title I funds to a much greater degree than they did ten years ago.

Despite this general record of improvement, federal administrative practices are not without some weaknesses. In fact, as a recent study of Title I administrative practices produced by the National Institute of Education (NIE) has documented, there are certain problems in each of the four functional areas of the administrative system.[2] In the next four sections, this essay will discuss

[1] U.S., Congress, House, Committee on Education and Labor, *Part 18: Administration of Title I of ESEA, Hearings before the Subcommittee on Elementary, Secondary, and Vocational Education*, 95th Cong., 1st sess., 1977 (Washington, D.C.: GPO, 1978), p. 6.

[2] Donald Burnes et al., *Administration of Compensatory Education* (Washington, D.C.: NIE, 1977).

these weaknesses and analyze some of the efforts being made to correct the faults. The final section will provide a more general examination of Title I and the federal role in education.

Rule-making

The rules governing the Title I program contained in the legal framework represent a vital mechanism by which the federal government articulates its policies and their interpretations to states and districts. Because they are central to the nature of the federal direction, it is important that these rules be clear to those who must make use of them. Although the regulations are internally consistent and do not conflict with the statute itself, the legal framework is not sufficiently clear to many of the state and local officials that rely on it. Substantial time, legal expertise, and field experience are all necessary for adequate understanding. Because many Title I directors have not had sufficient time to study the framework, they have great difficulty in comprehending all the regulations, guidelines, and interpretations.

Part of the reason for the lack of clarity stems from the way in which the legal framework has been constructed. It has developed over time on a case-by-case basis, with individual provisions created to address individual problems as they arose. There has been little effort to integrate all the rules into a unified whole, or, in the case of interpretations, to eliminate elements that have been superseded. The result is a complex patchwork of regulations and interpretations that frequently mystify even the most astute.

A second factor contributing to the lack of clarity is the OE's use of the framework to guide local activity. The framework contains two basic sets of rules. The first, related to the allocation of funds, ensures that Title I dollars are used to provide services for the intended beneficiaries and that state and local funds are distributed so that Title I dollars actually add to expenditures for the target population. These rules include provisions concerned with the selection of students who are to benefit from Title I, the prohibition of the use of Title I funds for general aid to all students in the district, the requirement that districts maintain their current fiscal effort, the provisions that services in Title I schools be comparable to those in other schools before the addition of Title I funds, and requirements that Title I services supplement those that students would otherwise have received. Without these regulations, local districts would have strong incentives to use these federal dollars for other purposes, such as general aid or tax relief.

The second type of rules concerning the planning and delivery of educational services is intended to ensure that the needs of the target children are addressed and that the programs are carefully planned, implemented, and evaluated. These rules include provisions that a district design programs to address the needs of Title I children who have been specifically identified, a requirement that the Title I program be coordinated with other federal and state programs, a provision that funds not be distributed to so many children that there is little likelihood that the services will have an impact, regulations requiring that the program be evaluated, and requirements that parents be involved in planning, implementing, and evaluating the program.

Although these rules constitute a sound, common-sense approach to program planning and development, they are not "necessary" in the same sense as the fund allocation requirements. Local districts are not under pressure to deliver bad programs. Nor is there sufficient knowledge about program design or evaluation in education to warrant the mandating of specific procedures and processes. Therefore, in placing extensive requirements on local districts about the design, implementation, and evaluation of Title I programs, the federal government is providing greater direction than necessary and is probably being more prescriptive than existing educational research data justify. In addition, even if districts follow the procedures laid out in the requirements, there is no guarantee that they will produce high-quality services. Moreover, many of the program development rules are less clear than the funds allocation requirements. States and local districts request clarification of the rules governing the design and implementation of programs far more frequently than they do of those about the allocation of funds, and many of the conflicts between OE and states and districts center on issues of program development.

It appears, then, that the federal government may be overusing its rule-making function. OE's attempts to control program quality through the creation of formal rules and requirements have resulted instead in increased confusion.

The lack of clarity in the legal framework can also be traced, in some cases, to disagreement within OE about the extent of federal intervention that is justified in Title I. Because of such internal conflict, rule-makers have occasionally had to develop carefully crafted compromises in the writing of certain regulations in order to obtain internal approval. These compromises, rather than providing clear, straightforward direction, have frequently created additional confusion for states and local districts.

Dissemination

Closely related to the rule-making function is the task of dissemination. If federal direction of states and districts is to be effective, rules must not only be clear, but they must also be widely disseminated. Problems in OE's performance of this function are similar to those in rule-making. Efforts to disseminate the rules, either through oral presentations, written communication, or responses to questions, are piecemeal. Interpretations are provided for specific issues and solutions suggested for specific problems, but little attempt is made to identify the underlying rationale for the rules or the relationship between one rule and several related ones. In addition, examples of exemplary practice are only infrequently provided.

To make matters worse, the available interpretative responses are not disseminated widely. Information in response to a question is sent only to the inquirer. It has been over ten years since OE has made an effort to collect the various interpretations of the legal framework and to disseminate them in a single volume to all the states and districts. Consequently, individuals in the field seldom have a full picture of the general direction of Title I policy, nor are they always aware of what they do not know.

One solution to the problems in rule-making and dissemination would be the development of a Title I policy manual. Such a document would assemble all of the regulations, guidelines, and interpretations and reorganize them into a unified whole. It would provide models of how to develop programs in compliance with the more complex rules. Because it is central to the way in which the federal government provides direction, it should also be widely circulated.

Despite its desirability, a policy manual will be completed only after a long and difficult period. Although some officials in OE have started the process of writing a manual, there is too much disagreement within OE and HEW about the federal role in education to offer much hope that a complete policy manual will be written and approved soon. Only through external pressure, like that emanating from a recent congressional mandate for such a manual, will the department write and broadly disseminate a clear and uncomplicated policy manual in the foreseeable future.

In addition, the creation of a policy manual would not resolve the problem of the overreliance on rule-making to provide direction for designing and implementing quality programs. In order to accomplish this, federal officials will have to reexamine the existing legal framework to determine which program development provisions are necessary or justified on the basis of educational research. The officials will also have to play a greater role in helping local districts, since informed technical assistance will do far more for the quality of Title I programs than continued efforts to legislate planning, implementation, and evaluation processes.

Monitoring

The difficulties created by the lack of clarity and inadequate dissemination of the legal framework are compounded as OE and the HEW Audit Agency perform their monitoring and enforcement functions. Within OE, officials inconsistently apply different standards as they monitor the same requirements, particularly with regard to the provisions that districts not use Title I funds to replace the regular instruction of Title I children. The differing standards reflect divergent views about the appropriate role of the federal government in guaranteeing the supplementary nature of Title I services. Some OE officials, who see Title I as basically a mechanism for distributing dollars, do not feel that the federal government should be active in ensuring that funds be used to provide supplementary services. Others argue that OE should make every effort to guarantee that the services supplement those already offered. As a result of this conflict, the overall federal effort to monitor these provisions has declined, and when officials do examine state and local behavior on this point, they provide unclear or inconsistent direction.

This inconsistency within OE is exacerbated by a lack of coordination between OE and the HEW Audit Agency in the conduct of formal audits. A fundamental disagreement over the purpose of the audits underlies this problem of coordination. Auditors, on the one hand, tend to view themselves as management analysts. Through careful examination of management practices at the state and local levels, they hope to identify mechanisms for improving Title I administration. OE program staff, on the other hand, view audits as a way of policing the system by uncovering instances of noncompliance and thus providing a means of recovering misspent Title I funds.

The following example highlights this difference. On the basis of a program review, OE staff identified a clear instance of noncompliance in one state. They requested that the Audit Agency conduct an audit in order to register a formal audit exception and thus start the process toward possibly recovering misspent federal dollars. The response of a senior auditor was, "Why should we have to do an audit when OE already knows the problem? Why can't they handle their own problems?" Under these circumstances, according to the auditors, an audit would not produce additional information that could be used to improve Title I management.

Further inconsistencies have developed between OE and the Audit Agency over the interpretation of the legal framework. Auditors review statutory requirements, legislative histories, regulations, and other parts of the legal framework in order to comprehend congressional intent. Based on their understanding, they identify for review particular areas of the framework as the most important for achieving the overall program goals. However, the interpretations of the auditors are not always consistent with those of OE. This would be true even if OE officials were in total agreement about the meaning of various rules.

Because of the differences between the Audit Agency and OE about the role of audits in the federal management of Title I and about interpretations of the legal framework, Title I audit activity has apparently declined. In many regions of the country, auditors are less likely now to conduct audits of Title I than in previous years; in one region, there has not been a new Title I audit in three years. Furthermore, when audits are conducted, audit exceptions focus more on procedural problems than on misuses of funds.

The lack of clarity in federal direction extends into another set of issues related to the exercise of the monitoring functions—the role of states in overseeing local district performance. Despite the important role that states are supposed to play in this area, many have not had a clear understanding of the extent of their monitoring responsibilities. The federal monitoring system has never been intended to serve as an oversight mechanism for all 14,000 Title I school districts. Federal program reviews and audits are conducted for the purpose of observing state practices. Visits to local districts are made in each case to verify state behavior, not as an independent check on local districts. Furthermore, federal monitoring resources are inadequate to mount a comprehensive monitoring system for all districts having these programs, nor is it likely that Congress would provide such resources. Rather, states have been given the primary administrative responsibility for monitoring the behavior of local school districts. They are supposed to make regular, systematic inspections of district practices and see that an audit of each district's program is conducted at least every two years.

However, despite the overall structure of the Title I management system and the importance of the state role, the federal legal framework is not clear in describing state responsibilities. For example, there are no clear standards explaining how states are to conduct audits, nor are there clear requirements about the nature and extent of state monitoring. State authority to enforce some of the Title I requirements is even more ambiguous, particularly the authority to withhold or suspend funds.

Differences in state attitudes regarding the desirability of state involvement in monitoring and enforcement accompany the lack of clarity in the rules. Some states have a strong tradition of local control in education. Because the federal legal framework does not provide clear direction about the nature and extent of state involvement, state education departments play a rather inactive role in overseeing local Title I activity in these states. In one of them, for example, state monitors visited less than 5 percent of the Title I districts in one year. In other states, where the state government has been active in education for years, administration is much more vigorous. In these states, monitoring visits are made to each district at least once every two years. State officials are also much more careful in ensuring that audits are conducted with the required frequency.

Differences in state attitudes toward involvement in oversight activity are reflected in their use of Title I funds for state administrative purposes. Although there is a formula for how much each state will receive for state administrative purposes, there is no direction for spending these funds. The NIE study on Title I administration, however, suggests that states more committed to an active state role use more of their state administrative funds to hire staff. Thus they are able to engage in staff-intensive activities at the state level—such as careful review of local district program plans and extensive on-site monitoring—that seem to have the greatest impact on local district performance.

The passage of the Title I legislation by Congress in 1978 should correct several of the current problems in federal monitoring of the program. New statutory provisions will clarify areas of disagreement within OE about the supplementary nature of the program. Perhaps more important, the new law is much more specific about the role that states are to play in the administration of Title I.

However, if the Title I program is to be completely successful in creating a management system that is comprehensive in its oversight of local districts, it must do more than clarify the law. In light of the significant differences among states in their commitment to playing an active role, a more extensive system of incentives may have to be established to convince some states that aggressive monitoring is in their best interest.

Enforcement

By any standard, federal enforcement activities have had a substantial impact on Title I programs across the country. The degree of compliance with federal regulations has increased dramatically since the early years of the program. Furthermore, observers of state and local administration of Title I have independently noted the impact of the audit process and the sanctions that result. As one observer remarked, "The HEW audit process is the single most important aspect of the Federal role in promoting state attention [to the legal framework]."[3] In fact, the threat of an audit exception has created such a strong fear among states and districts that some unintended consequences have resulted. In the absence of clear guidance about legally acceptable and unacceptable programs, many local district officials have interpreted the rules in the most conservative and restrictive way in order to avoid any possibility of an audit exception. As a consequence, creativity and imagination in program planning have suffered.

For example, the federal legal framework provides that services can be delivered to Title I children while they are in their regular classroom or when they are "pulled out" in a separate location. However, because many local districts have historically found it easier to document that services are supplementary when the children are in a "pulled-out" class, most districts across the country do pull children out of the regular classroom to receive Title I services, even though few research data suggest this is a more effective teaching strategy. Other states prohibit other program design components, such as art or music instruction, guidance counselors, or health services, because such services have been prone to audit exceptions.

Another consequence is the increasing role that lawyers and accountants are playing in program decisions. Because of the lack of clarity in some of the regulations and the fear of audits, lawyers and accountants—not teachers and principals—are being asked to render final judgment on program plans, because they are the ones who will be responsible for contesting any negative findings from federal auditors.

The extent of the impact of the audits may be surprising when one considers that less than 1 percent of the funds identified as misspent through the initial findings of auditors has actually been returned to OE. However, states and districts appear to be extremely concerned about the local embarrassment caused by the publicity frequently given to audit exceptions. They also want to avoid the tedious, time-consuming, and expensive process they must undertake in order to contest an audit exception, regardless of the final outcome of the process. Thus the publicity that an initial negative audit finding attracts and the

[3] Robert Goettel et al., *A Study of the Administration of the Elementary and Secondary Education Act, ESEA, Title I in Eight States* (Syracuse, N.Y.: Syracuse Research Corp., 1977), p. 144.

demands of the process that is required to contest findings of the auditors are, in and of themselves, substantial deterrents for many states and local districts.

Yet there is a certain lack of realism in the existing federal sanction structure as evidenced by the paltry percentage of funds returned to OE and by present efforts to modify it. One problem is the extremely severe penalties for noncompliance. A minor infraction of the regulations in one school building can jeopardize an entire district's Title I grant for a considerable period of time. There is no way at present to gear the sanction to the extent of the infraction or to phase it in over time.

In addition, OE has strong incentives not to apply the available sanctions. As one analyst put it, "The essential problem with the sanctions that are available to OE is that they are counter productive because they decrease the capacity to deliver services."[4] The imposition of the federal Title I sanction reduces the overall supply of resources that a state or district has to expend on education.

In addition, OE must bear great political costs in withholding funds or in demanding their return. Much of OE's activity administering programs is designed to create and nurture a variety of educational constituencies throughout the country. The imposition of strong sanctions can be detrimental to the maintenance of vital components of the Title I constituency.

The new congressional mandate for Title I of ESEA contains a partial solution to some of the failings in these areas of enforcement. The new system being considered would permit a one-year interval between the identification of an abuse of the rules and the demand for repayment of funds, if the abuse is corrected during that year. This strategy would more closely reflect existing incentives and pressures in OE and therefore would probably be utilized more extensively. Even here, however, a reduction of funds available for education constitutes the ultimate threat. Also needed is consideration of positive fiscal incentives appealing enough to persuade states and districts to correct the weaknesses in their administration of the program.

Title I and the Federal Role

Even after twelve years of Title I operations there are several weaknesses in the program. The rules are not always clear, nor are they well disseminated. Efforts to monitor compliance with rules are inconsistent and uncoordinated. The system of sanctions available in cases of noncompliance is far from ideal.

These faults do not indicate the need for a massive overhaul of the program. Although certain improvements could be made in the system, some of which have been described here, the imperfections do not negate the basic importance of the system. If the federal government wishes to provide special supplementary programs for disadvantaged children, a federal management structure, not un-

---

[4] Paul Hill, "Federal Management Tools for Categorical Programs" (Paper delivered at the 30th Annual Meeting of the Northwest Political Science Association, Seattle, Washington, April 28, 1978), p. 16.

like the present one, is necessary. Only if the Title I legislation were intended to authorize a program of general aid for poor areas, could federal management be altered significantly.

Some critics interested in Title I as a program of general aid have advocated the abolition of virtually the entire legal framework. They have argued that local districts, unencumbered by federal rules and red tape, would improve programs for disadvantaged children. Others demand an elimination of federal efforts to monitor and enforce the Title I legal framework and claim that Washington can only stultify local creativity and ingenuity in education and thus should be eliminated.

Although there is no direct empirical evidence of what Title I would look like if Congress and HEW implemented these proposals *in toto*, various data indicate the possible future of Title I if the present federal management structure were significantly weakened. The early history of Title I is one indication. As reported earlier, OE functioned essentially as a check-writing operation in the first several years of Title I. Few rules existed and even fewer efforts to enforce those rules were in evidence, resulting in massive noncompliance and widespread malfeasance. The use of Title I funds as general aid was the rule, not the exception.

Much has happened since the late 1960s. Many would argue that because of programs like Title I, there is now a much greater national commitment to providing educational services for disadvantaged children. In light of that increased commitment, the argument continues, the tight reins over local discretion in Title I can be relaxed. However, as many state and local officials indicated to NIE staff during the course of the Compensatory Education Study, relaxing the Title I requirements would only undermine district efforts to provide special assistance to disadvantaged children. Without the comprehensive regulations regarding the use of Title I funds, many state and local superintendents would be unable to resist the strong fiscal pressures to use these federal dollars for general aid or as tax relief. As one local official stated: "We cannot finance remedial programs locally; we have to do it through state and Federal dollars. . . . We have to ensure that the federal categorical grant process does not become block grant because [the funds would be distributed without regard to need for compensatory education]. The Title I program in the state of . . . works. . . . If you want to see that continued in the state of . . . , then do not change Title I from categorical to block grant."

A third indication of the likely outcome of a major change in the Title I management structure is provided by state efforts to fund compensatory education. As of FY 1976, sixteen states spent almost $365 million for disadvantaged children. Unlike Title I, however, these programs are initiated at the state level through the state legislative process and can therefore be viewed as a barometer of what compensatory education would be like without a strong federal presence.

Although many of these programs provide funds for educational services similar to those funded under Title I, there is a significant difference between Title I and many of these programs. Unlike Title I, there is no strong commitment to providing supplementary services for disadvantaged children. In some states, the compensatory education program is little more than a statutory vehicle for providing additional general funds to some districts. In many cases where state rules are explicit about the supplementary nature of the program, there is virtually no mechanism for ensuring that certain children receive special, additional services. Monitoring and enforcement of the state rules are minimal, if not nonexistent.

These observations provide strong evidence for the desirable degree of federal involvement in Title I. A system that consists of making rules about the use of federal dollars, broadly disseminating those rules, and monitoring and enforcing their compliance is needed if the present intent of Congress is to be met. Most federal, state, and local officials have come to accept the intent of Title I and the need for a federal Title I management system. Calls for change in that system are not demands for a wholesale dismantling of the entire structure but for modifications of particular features that seem unworkable.

The recent history of Title I suggests that the federal system is remarkably responsive to these calls for change. For example, the statute has undergone considerable modification in order to address the concerns of state and local officials about rules relating to the maintenance of fiscal effort (provisions that require school districts to maintain prior levels of state and local funding). The new law also contains changes suggested by recent research on Title I and by comments from states and districts. Within OE, policies about appropriate sanctions in cases involving the comparability of services in Title I and non-Title I schools are being modified in response to research findings and the concerns of state and local officials.

Such changes, however, do not constitute a fundamental overhaul of the Title I program. That kind of change is unlikely in the foreseeable future. In fact, the ability of the federal system to respond to empirical research and to the concerns of state and local officials reduces the likelihood of a large scale redirection of the federal management system. In short, Title I, as a program of special educational services for disadvantaged children with federal management tools to implement it, will continue for some time to come.

This essay was written by Donald Burnes in his private capacity. No official support or endorsement by the National Institute of Education or by the Department of Health, Education, and Welfare is intended or should be inferred.

Education of the Handicapped

JANET M. SIMONS
BARBARA DWYER

Local responsibility for education is a long-standing tradition in the United States. Despite increasing federal support for education over the past two decades, state and local education agencies, their staffs, and teachers have determined educational policy. Until recently, education of the handicapped, or special education, followed this pattern. Legislation passed by Congress in 1975 has had a great impact on this traditional balance.

State legislation mandating public education for the handicapped dates back to the New Jersey legislation of 1954. By 1970, eleven states had adopted such legislation; by 1976, an additional thirty-eight states had passed similar laws. Two 1972 court cases, however, illustrated that education for all handicapped children was still not a guaranteed right. *PARC* v. *Pennsylvania* held that the state could not deny a public education to retarded children; *Mills* v. *Board of Education* (in the District of Columbia) extended this principle to include all handicapped children.

The federal government responded with section 504 of the Rehabilitation Act of 1973, which stated: "No otherwise qualified handicapped individual in the United States . . . shall, solely by reason of his handicap, be excluded from participation in, be denied the benefits of, or be subjected to discrimination under any program or activity receiving Federal financial assistance." Despite this strong language, the act provided no funds to implement this mandate, and regulations were not promulgated until 1977. Although funding for special education came with the Education Amendments of 1974, a greater effort was needed. The best information available to Congress in October 1975, when the Education for All Handicapped Children Act (PL 94–142) was passed, indicated that there were more than 8 million handicapped children in the United States, that more than half of these children were not receiving appropriate educational services, and that fully 1 million handicapped children were excluded entirely from the public school system. Before the act was passed, few "due process"

The order in which the names of the authors of this essay appear is not intended to reflect their relative contributions.

guarantees existed for handicapped children, who could be excluded from school without cause. A few states, of course, had these protections, but they varied greatly. Some families could provide adequate educational services for their handicapped children in private facilities, often at great cost and in facilities far from their communities. Other families were unable to educate their handicapped children. These and other factors led to the passage of the act.

Perhaps because of a long history of insufficient special education legislation, federal intervention seemed essential at this point. The Education for All Handicapped Children Act is the first time the federal government has so precisely defined instructional style, the rights of parents and children to due process, and state and local responsibilities for monitoring instruction. To satisfy the mandates of this multifaceted legislation, state and local education agencies have had to modify significantly their organizational, administrative, behavioral, and attitudinal practices.

During the complex process of implementing a federal law, however, the intent of the law may be significantly changed or lost. The multiple goals of some legislation, such as PL 94–142, often lead to changes unintended by the law that may overwhelm its original intent. Richard Weatherley and Michael Lipsky have described implementation, in part, as "the substantial unintended modification of the law resulting from the efforts of school personnel to accommodate to additional and conflicting requirements."[1] Implementation additionally results in change unintended by the federal law but that state or local education agencies bring about by using the weight of the federal law to achieve their own political or philosophical goals. Both types of unintended change are important.

This essay will examine some of the unintended changes that occurred in state and local education agencies during the first two years of the implementation of PL 94–142. Special attention will be given to the impact of a federal initiative beyond the stated intent of the law, areas in which state and local education agencies are making unnecessary modifications that impede implementation, and trends that may need to be corrected to ensure full implementation. First, however, the major elements of PL 94–142 can be briefly stated.

In a sense, the law incorporates features of previous legislation and adds a few new ones. Its purpose is "to assure that all handicapped children have available to them . . . a free appropriate public education which emphasizes special education and related services designed to meet their unique needs, to assure that the rights of handicapped children and their parents or guardians are protected, to assist states and localities to provide for the education of all handicapped children." The act also defines in detail a number of elements that are contained within the broad concept of "free appropriate public education."

According to the regulations issued to implement the law, state and local education agencies must first identify all handicapped children within their

[1] Richard Weatherley and Michael Lipsky, "Street-level Bureaucrats and Institutional Innovation: Implementing Special-Education Reform in Education" (Paper delivered at the 72d Annual Meeting of the American Political Science Association, Chicago, September 1976), p. 2.

jurisdictions, a process referred to as "childfind." Two categories of children are singled out: first priority children, currently unserved; and second priority children, severely handicapped children who are inadequately served. States must actively seek out handicapped children through a variety of media.

Once children who may be handicapped have been identified, they must be assessed, which includes testing. The regulations require that this be done in a nondiscriminatory manner: diagnosis cannot be based on a single test result, testing must be done by trained, qualified personnel, and tests must be selected so as not to be racially or culturally discriminatory. Further, tests must be administered in a child's primary language or major mode of communication.

Placement of handicapped children must be in the least restrictive environment. Although this does not mean that all handicapped children are to be placed in a regular classroom for all or part of their education, it does mean that they are to be educated with nonhandicapped children to the maximum extent possible, consistent with the achievement of goals set for these children. This could mean, for example, that handicapped children may be in regular classes for art, music, and physical education and in separate classes for other, academic work. Other children—those with minor speech defects, for instance—may spend all but an hour or two a week in regular classes. Still others—the severely or multiple handicapped, for example—may spend all their school days in separate classes or separate buildings.

Each child diagnosed as handicapped must have an individualized education program (IEP). This is one of the major innovative elements of the law. The many components of an IEP are detailed in the legislation (section 4):

> The term "individualized education program" means a written statement for each handicapped child developed in any meeting by a representative of the local educational agency or an intermediate educational unit who shall be qualified to provide, or supervise the provision of, specially designed instruction to meet the unique needs of handicapped children, the teacher, the parents or guardian of such child, and, whenever appropriate, such child, which statement shall include (a) a statement of the present levels of educational performance of such child, (b) a statement of annual goals, including short-term instructional objectives, (c) a statement of the specific educational services to be provided to such child, and the extent to which such child will be able to participate in regular educational programs, (d) the projected date for initiation and anticipated duration of such services, and (e) appropriate objective criteria and evaluation procedures and schedules for determining, on at least an annual basis, whether instructional objectives are being achieved.

The regulations required that IEPs must have been developed for all children receiving special education services by October 1, 1977, and that all IEPs must be reviewed at least annually.

Partly because of the influence of advocacy groups, the law and the regulations place a great deal of emphasis on due process and on parental involvement. Parents must be fully informed about all procedures relating to their children, including evaluation and placement, and must be given notice before any procedures can be undertaken. Parents must consent in writing to such procedures;

if a parent refuses consent, the federal law defers to state policy to determine what recourse the local district or the state has. Parents have the right to appeal any decisions made about their children; hearings on these appeals must be conducted by impartial hearing officers—individuals who are not otherwise employed by the agency making the decision.

Another major innovation of the law is that state education agencies (SEAs) have a major responsibility to supervise all educational services provided to the handicapped by other state agencies. In most states, direct services to the handicapped are provided by a variety of agencies, including departments of mental health, mental retardation, health, youth services, and corrections. Henceforth, the educational components of these programs must be conducted under the supervision of or monitored by the SEA, even though funds and staff may be provided by other agencies.

This federal legislation authorizes funds as well as guaranteeing a free appropriate public education. The level of funding that a state receives is determined by three factors: the number of handicapped children in the state, the national average per pupil expenditure, and a percentage specified in the act. Thus, a state's allocation is determined by multiplying the per pupil average expenditure by the appropriate percentage and then multiplying that amount by the number of handicapped children in the state. For the school year 1977–78, the appropriate percentage was 5 percent; for 1978–79, 10 percent; for 1979–80, 20 percent; for 1980–81, 30 percent; and for 1981–82 and every year thereafter, 40 percent.

Several unintended changes have resulted from the act, primarily at the local level but also to some degree at the state level. Most of the data were collected over the past two years in projects funded by the U.S. Office of Education, Bureau of Education for the Handicapped. One project studied the perceptions of state and local personnel of the individualized education program in four states. Others studied parental involvement in the special education process and examined the effects of mainstreaming. Additional data were collected in a study of state education agency supervision of services for the handicapped that was conducted in three states for the National Conference of State Legislatures. None of the states or districts involved in these studies will be identified, in order to protect the anonymity of respondents.

The reader should keep in mind that these observations are based on only ten school districts and seven states. The examples are not generalizable to all districts or all states, but rather merely illustrate reactions to a federal law in the early stages of implementation.

The Individualized Education Program (IEP)

The IEP component of the law had the earliest impact on state and local education agencies, partly because IEPs had to be developed before other provisions of the law were implemented and partly because for the first time the federal government defined educational style for states and localities. The IEP must contain detailed objectives for instruction; it must also reflect a group planning effort. Furthermore, the IEP must contain information related to most of the major assurances of the law: data on assessment procedures, on the multidisciplinary team that developed the IEP, on placement, and on due process procedures. Lastly, the IEP must serve as a compliance document; state education agencies must annually evaluate IEPs prepared by local education agencies, and local agencies must be able to prove that IEPs exist for all handicapped children.

Patricia A. Morrissey and Nancy Safer theorize that the IEP can therefore be used as "a planning system for instructional service delivery and documentation which should facilitate service to the individual handicapped child and contribute to the provision of a general record of the allocation and use of special education and related services."[2]

This new, multipurpose document leaves state and local education agencies with a requirement to implement change at several levels. Because the IEPs had to be prepared for all handicapped children within two months of the promulgation of the regulations, however, the compliance element became the primary focus of the IEP in its first year of implementation. The first unintended impact of implementing the law in the districts studied was the development of a standard IEP format that was used by all schools. In all these districts, including those that had an IEP-type planning process in place before the law was passed, school officials believed that developing a standard format and language for IEPs was necessary for compliance with the law. It does not in fact require conformity in language or format; rather, state education agencies urged their local agencies to standardize their documents, in part to ease the state's monitoring burden (an unintended political change linked to the mandate), and local officials believed standard language was part of compliance requirements.

Several other unintended impacts resulted from this standardization process. To demonstrate compliance, local education agencies used the IEP as a planning system, as Morrissey and Safer had suggested could occur. The use of the IEP as a compliance document, however, has not diminished its value as a planning document. In the local education agencies studied, most IEPs were four to five pages long and contained information related to all the major assurances of the law. At the group meetings held to discuss assessment or placement, the IEP is the major reference document because it contains all the available information on the handicapped child. Many local education agencies never before kept all these data in one place; they now find it easier to plan programs and more difficult to "lose" a child who transfers from one class to another or from one school to another. The IEP also becomes the agenda for group planning meetings and helps staff provide more consistent service to children. Regular teachers in one district, for example, now refer to the IEP document filed in the guidance counselor's office when planning course work for their pupils. To col-

[2] Patricia A. Morrissey and Nancy Safer, "Implications for Special Education: The Individualized Education Program," *Viewpoints* 53 (March 1977): 32.

lect all the information necessary to meet the PL 94–142 assurances and to complete the lengthy IEP document, however, often requires several separate group meetings for each handicapped child. In one district, staff, teachers, administrators, and parents meet up to five times to develop one child's IEP.

Unfortunately, when the IEP is seen primarily as a monitoring document, its use as an instructional tool is diminished. Those schools with no tradition of individualized instruction like that described in a child's IEP often have not absorbed the IEP into their classroom routine. Special education teachers view IEP development as an additional clerical task unrelated to instruction. They often have only ten days after long-term goals have been established for a child to write short-term objectives; they then submit the IEP to the central office and, often with no copying machine available, do not keep a copy themselves. The IEP is thus filed and forgotten until an annual or compliance review.

As a result of continued, early emphasis on the IEP as a monitoring tool, it may serve neither an instructional nor a monitoring purpose very effectively. Some teachers, fearful of being held accountable for a child's progress, may write general objectives rather than specific short-term ones. Some teachers asserted that they are unsure how to write short-term objectives. One district admitted that it never lists a long-term goal unless the services are available in the district.

The implementation of the IEP has had another early and unintended impact. Preparation of these long forms has sidetracked many districts from the task of improving services to the handicapped. Most districts studied spent a significant portion, if not all, of their early federal grant monies to set up a system for writing, copying, and mailing the IEP forms to parents rather than to hire instructional staff or buy instructional materials. One district purchased a word processor to free teachers from the task of writing short-term objectives. In another district, most of the staff hired were clerical personnel, secretaries to type IEPs and mail forms and letters of notification to parents, staff to arrange meetings, and central office staff to coordinate activities among regular and special education staff and with outside agencies that serve handicapped children.

In several local districts in one state, processing of the "paper system" was frequently assigned to school psychologists, guidance counselors, or social workers—special education support staff—who spent most of their time completing IEP forms, arranging group meetings for completing the forms, and contacting parents. These staff complained that they had little time for their regular duties, such as counseling nonhandicapped children or testing handicapped children. Again, all this time devoted to maintaining records is deemed essential to demonstrate compliance with the federal legislation.

Yet another impact of the compliance requirement of the IEP is that they are often prepared in group meetings that involve ten to fifteen staff people and parents. Local districts believe that, to follow the intent of the law, all staff who have had contact with a child must participate in these meetings. Although these large groups intimidate parents and take a great deal of staff time, the process has had some beneficial effects. Educators have had unprecedented opportunities to discuss program changes together; program insufficiencies appear more readily when staff consistently review the needs of children with similar problems. Additionally, for the first time in most districts, regular teachers are involved in special education programming. They admit that they now better appreciate the role of the special education teacher. In several districts, staff felt that their roles were more precisely defined as a result of the tasks assigned because of PL 94-142 requirements. Efforts are not duplicated as often when one staff person is assigned to a specific task.

Due Process

The local education agencies studied have also developed more systematic procedures for guaranteeing due process, again initially focusing on compliance issues. Because the federal law requires that schools notify parents at every stage of the special education process—before testing and other assessment procedures, during IEP development, and before placement in a special program—some school systems have overreacted by requiring numerous signatures by parents. Despite this emphasis, a parent's signature may indicate neither knowledge nor understanding of decisions that have been made about a child.

Local education agency staffs have also spent a great deal of time formally inviting parents to meetings, scheduling meetings, hiring translators for non-English-speaking parents, and arranging for transportation for parents to meetings. But parents may nevertheless come to these meetings uninformed of the program options available for their children, intimidated by the large number of professionals at the meeting, and unsure of what instruction their children will receive, even though they consent to and sign the IEP.

An unexpected effect of parental involvement is that some schools are concerned about the level of effort necessary to contact parents and to obtain consent at all appropriate junctures. The local districts studied were unsure if sufficient resources were available to maintain intense home-school involvement, such as sending staff to homes to obtain parental approval or evaluating the home environment when determining a special education diagnosis. Neither is specifically required by the federal law, but some local districts assume they are necessary. However, the benefits of local activity in this area are slowly appearing. In one district, parents noted that, in the second year of implementation, they felt more comfortable participating in program discussions about their children.

Fiscal Impacts at the Local Level

The federal law has of necessity had a major fiscal impact at both the state and local levels. Because the law is directed at improving programs for the handicapped in local districts, increased costs are implicit in the legislation. Nevertheless, unintended impacts that could modify the intent of the law accrue as states and localities juggle budgets and make decisions about what to fund first. To achieve compliance, local districts often required increases in their special education budgets of 50 percent to 100 percent in the first implementation year, primarily to hire personnel. Nevertheless, the modifications these districts have made in their programs are still not what local administrators feel is necessary to comply with the law. These expenditures are the result of local perceptions of what compliance means and can lead to many unintended effects.

One unintended impact has been an attitudinal one. Many of the parents of nonhandicapped children and some board members believe that special education is diverting resources from regular programs. The special education budget continues to increase rapidly while other elements of the school budget grow much more slowly or have been reduced. These perceived inequities lead to morale problems. Administrators and regular education teachers resent the increased power of the special education program.

Special education costs in local education agencies (LEAs) will probably continue to rise, however, as local districts begin to reclaim and educate handicapped children formerly placed in institutions or other settings outside school buildings. For example, special education programs in many districts, particularly small ones, are inadequate to provide services for all their handicapped children. Such small districts are unlikely to have enough children with a low-incidence handicap (e.g., deaf-blind or other multihandicapped children) to warrant starting a program. They are therefore entering into cooperative arrangements with other districts to provide services, or finding placements at private facilities, within or outside the district. In either case, the local district sending the students will pay transportation costs and tuition and may also have to pay for room and board for students who live too far away for daily commuting.

State funding formulas can have an unintended influence on where handicapped children are placed. In some states, the formula encourages keeping the children in regular classrooms while in others it rewards LEAs for placing handicapped children in segregated classes. A recent report by the New York City Comptroller's Office, for example, found that it costs the city less to place handicapped children in private schools than to educate them in the public schools because of the state reimbursement formula.[3]

In some states, other public agencies may place handicapped children in private facilities and then bill the appropriate LEA for the cost; the LEA has usually not been involved in the decision-making process for the child. Various local agencies argue over who is responsible for providing services to handicapped children. Many of these agencies—such as the departments of health, mental health, and youth services—have concluded that the federal act makes the local district financially responsible for services that it previously received without cost.

[3] *New York Times*, June 18, 1978.

Impacts at the State Level

As noted above, one of the innovations of the federal act is the requirement that the state education agency (SEA) supervise the delivery of educational services to the handicapped, even though these services might be provided by other state agencies. In response, many states have drawn up memorandums of collaboration between the SEA and these other agencies, while the state education agency often contracts with other state agencies to provide services.

Another approach is the creation of a special school district that encompasses all state-run institutions within the state. All noneducational services remain under the control of the relevant parent agencies, but education is the responsibility solely of this statewide school district (SWSD). All teachers are employees of the SWSD, whereas previously they were employed by the agencies that run the institutions.

There are some obvious problems in this approach. The SEA is, in effect, taking over major portions of programs previously run by other agencies. This means that these agencies lose staff and budget, which is contrary to the nature of bureaucracies. One of the prime functions of almost any bureaucracy is system maintenance. The SWSD still has to work with these other agencies, however. Officials in one SWSD commented that this was very difficult, and that they frequently had to ask other agencies for help when coordination of services was necessary. Such coordination was most effective through informal contacts with officials in other agencies. This creation of a formal mechanism in response to the federal act may not have resulted in an actual reduction in services to the handicapped, but it has slowed their delivery. A positive outcome of these SWSDs is that, in some states, handicapped children in state institutions now receive educational services. Before these districts were created, these children often received no education at all; the institutions served merely as caretakers, feeding, clothing, and housing the handicapped.

The act also requires state education agencies to monitor and evaluate the IEPs developed by the local districts within the state. Specifically, the state agency must randomly select a sample of IEPs every year and evaluate them against the services provided to the children. One federal official noted that, one year after this provision of the law went into effect, only three states at the most complied with this requirement.

Conclusion

The federal act has been hailed as a bill of rights for the handicapped. In many ways this is true; handicapped children are now guaranteed the same right to a free public education that nonhandicapped children have enjoyed for years. But this "free" education costs a great deal of money. In New York City, for instance, per pupil costs for multihandicapped children were as high as $13,900 in

1975 and are probably even higher now.[4] In contrast, the per pupil allocation under the act that was actually passed through to local districts in 1977–78 was only slightly more than $35. This comparison is, of course, extreme, but it does illustrate a point: there were few financial incentives for local districts to implement the law on schedule, by September 1, 1978. Appropriations are supposed to escalate over a five-year period, but there are indications that this will not take place as authorized in the law. The president's budget for FY 1979 called for funding at only the 12 percent level for the 1979–80 school year, rather than the 20 percent authorized in the legislation. Congress did not increase the appropriation.

There are, however, some incentives to implementation. For example, state and local education agencies are afraid of being sued by parents or by advocacy groups if they do not provide the free appropriate public education as stipulated in the act. Partly with this in mind, states and local districts are implementing the law to the best of their ability, given their limited resources, their many obligations under the law, and the burden of paperwork imposed by the law and the regulations.

Perhaps the most important incentives are professional and personal. Almost everyone charged with responsibility under the act agrees with the intent of the law. Teachers, administrators, board members, and supporting staff generally have devoted a great deal of financially unrewarded effort to making the law work. It will probably be several years, however, before a majority of the local districts in the United States have smoothly functioning, quality special education programs that truly meet the goal of a free appropriate public education for all handicapped children.

Since the 1960s, federal officials have become more aware that, if federal innovations are to succeed at all, they must be accompanied by strong and timely support systems: funding, technical assistance, explanatory memorandums and guidelines, frequent communication, and program evaluations. PL 94–142 is highly innovative and also creates a stronger federal role in special education policy. Federal, state, and local officials must adjust to different responsibilities as the traditional balance of power in special education shifts toward the federal level. The examples in this essay of unintended change in, and unnecessary modifications of, local and state practices have identified areas where even greater communication and assistance are necessary between the federal government and state and local education agencies to achieve a quality education for all handicapped children.

---

[4] Bernard R. Gifford, *The Cost of Educating Handicapped Pupils in New York City* (New York: Board of Education of the City of New York, Office of the Deputy Chancellor, Educational Policy Analysis Unit, January 1977), p. 82.

Although the data from which this essay was drawn were collected primarily through projects funded by the U.S. Office of Education, Bureau of Education for the Handicapped, the opinions expressed herein are strictly those of the authors. No endorsement by the U.S. Office of Education is intended or implied. The authors would like to thank Maryann K. Hoff, Patricia A. Morrissey, and Nancy Safer for their helpful comments on an earlier draft of this essay.

Federal Attempts to
Change the Schools

BRUCE DOLLAR

In the past twenty years the federal government has enormously increased its monetary commitment both to schools and to research and development in an effort to change educational practice. The new federal involvement amounts to a sea change in its historical relationship to the nation's educational system. With schooling a legal responsibility of the states and a traditional outpost of local control, the federal role in education through the first half of this century was limited to a minor service function.

Beginning in the late 1950s, the federal role expanded steadily and exploded in scope in the mid-1960s, the "Education Decade." The biggest single contributor to this increase, both for categorical aid programs and for research and development, was the Elementary and Secondary Education Act of 1965 (ESEA), with $1.2 billion appropriated under all titles during the first year. Between 1963 and 1973, the annual budget of the U.S. Office of Education (OE) grew from $477 million to $5.5 billion, while over the same period attempts to improve school practice alone took some ten billion federal dollars.

The floodtide of new funds for education came in a climate of high expectations of their potential for bringing about desired changes not only in education but also in the society at large. The federal government became the chief sponsor of educational change, breaking long-standing tradition not merely by its new activist role but in some cases by seeking to deal directly with educators at the local level and bypassing state education agencies (SEAs). Innovation during these days of heady optimism was given so much attention, along with apparent public support and seemingly unlimited resources, that it became practically an end in itself. A huge R&D community was spawned as part of the process. It took years before reports on the impact of these efforts began to trickle back from the field, and the reports were not good. Only in recent years has reliable information become available to explain what went wrong. The experience has raised some vexing questions about the ability of the federal government to induce changes in education.

Federal Sponsorship of School Change

The watershed year for active federal intervention in education was 1965, the year that ESEA was passed. A fortuitous convergence of circumstances in the immediately preceding years had paved the way for a major break with tradition in the scope and the targets of federal aid to education. Far more than education alone figured in those circumstances. For these were the Great Society salad days, a time when it was widely believed that the federal government could become an engine for solving major social problems. With an eager Democratic majority in Congress, a robust, expanding economy, a bursting confidence in technology, and the best and the brightest at the controls, there seemed little that could hold back the government's benign juggernaut.

The need for federal leadership was an article of faith. The central government alone commanded the resources required by such a mammoth undertaking. Local and state governments could not be trusted to conform to nationally defined priorities. Education had been a particular focal point of desegregation efforts, giving state and local education authorities an obstructionist image in Washington. For these reasons, the logic of federal sponsorship of change appeared so compelling as to be virtually unquestioned.

Although many of the new federal programs such as ESEA, Headstart, and Project Follow-Through focused on education, it is important to note the extent to which they were motivated by noneducational concerns. As part of the Great Society's attack on poverty and discrimination, they are more properly viewed as broad-scale social action programs, with education as the vehicle for reaching social-political goals. The ostensible objective of increased educational achievement for poor and minority children was in reality a surrogate for the broader social changes that it was hoped would eventually flow from improved schooling.

Also behind the programs and the legislation was a constellation of more strictly political objectives. The legislative intent, as revealed in the relevant committee hearings and debates over ESEA Title I, for example, included a number of elements unrelated to the schools' ability to improve poor children's achievements. One of these involved a long-standing effort to win congressional acceptance of direct federal financial assistance for public schools; the objective for this was to establish a political precedent, not to increase achievement. Another factor was the hope of some legislators that federal money would act to dampen the rising political conflict over city schools at the time. Still another concerned the plight of the larger cities, which were experiencing population changes, a declining tax base, and rising service needs and costs. Municipal officials and educators saw the new aid scheme as an opportunity to ease pressures on their revenues.

Other federally sponsored educational programs shared many of the political purposes underlying Title I. These were carried out by a range of federal departments by no means limited to the OE or even Health, Education, and Welfare (HEW).

Education had become a major focus for a broad strategy to assert national priorities at the state and especially at the local levels. Whereas state education officials had always had maximum discretion in interpreting and implementing federal categorical laws, the new pattern of federal-to-local categorical grants tended to bypass the states and exert influence directly on local districts. The direct grants, it was thought, would tighten federal control over how the money was spent, in contrast to the previous practice of issuing general guidelines subject to interpretation by the states.

For educational policymakers and researchers, these programs were viewed as "natural experiments" that would provide badly needed knowledge about which kinds of programmatic approaches worked and which did not. From this point of view, compensatory education and other social action programs were undertaken, according to Alice Rivlin, in a study for the Brookings Institution, on the theory that "external resources spent to compensate for lack of intellectual stimulation at home would improve the performance of poor children in school and break the cycle of poverty. . . . The decision was to provide funds to local education systems for programs for poor children. The educators hoped for significant improvements in the average performance of poor children. The analyst hoped that something would be learned from the experience. Both have been largely disappointed."[1]

It is generally accepted that the results of federally sponsored educational change programs have been null. A study of the major evaluations of Title I, for example, confirmed the general verdict that it has failed as an instrument of national policy. Not one of the national evaluations was able to identify how participation in Title I programs or the expenditure of Title I funds had affected target children. Similarly, a long-awaited evaluation of the Follow-Through program, described as the largest and most expensive federal educational experiment in this country's history, found that "as a federal intervention strategy, Follow-Through was neither effective nor reliable" in meeting its central goal of improving the test scores of poor children.

In recent years, efforts to rectify or at least adequately explain the relentless negativism of these results have begun to focus on implementation. Rejecting interpretations that conclude that broad-scale change programs are ineffectual and ought to be abandoned, as well as those that maintain that further research and better technology are needed, those examining implementation suggest that the programs that suffer such disastrous evaluations have not failed so much as they have never been tried. They are "nontreatment programs."

It is important, however, not to lose sight of the ways these programs did succeed and of the goals and objectives that they fulfilled. On the broadest plane they succeeded in moving a lot of money to congressional constituencies back home, especially to local professionals and administrators, but also to poor local school districts where funds were short (a reflection of inequitable state

[1] Alice Rivlin, *Systematic Thinking for Social Action* (Washington, D.C.: The Brookings Institution, 1971), p. 84.

financing systems) and needs were high. Although modest in the overall scheme of school financing and local poverty, this redistributive effect was an important political goal for the national government. And of course attractive sums of money were disbursed to less needy constituencies as well. The programs also met the important basic goal of establishing the principle of an active federal presence in educational affairs, both in the form of "general" aid (which Title I was erroneously interpreted to be and, it may be argued, was its functional equivalent) and in the form of categorical aid for federally designated programs. Even more critical than the fact of federal aid to education was this opportunity to use the categorical grant system to assert federal prioritites on a decentralized system deeply rooted in traditions of localism.

Perhaps the most important effect of the expanded federal role in education was the way it defined the federal involvement in educational innovation. Both through its support of change programs and through its promotion of educational research and development, the federal government had become both the chief sponsor and chief consumer of educational innovation. This lock on the innovation market must be viewed as an important outcome of the overall federal effort in education, even if the benefits do not happen to include effective implementation of programs at the delivery level.

Barriers to Change

Analysts noting that federal change programs for the most part had not been implemented were quick to define the problem as one of local failure to comply with federal directives. Explanations for the resistance were immediately sought by focusing on conditions in local school districts. Easily overlooked, however, were conditions at the federal level that served to dissipate the federal initiatives.

In order for compliance with policy directives to be assured, a number of factors must be present in the relationship between policy makers and policy receivers. First, goals need to be shared and mutually understood. Second, there must be knowledge of three kinds: both must know what alternative actions can be effective; subordinates must know what is expected of them; and superiors must know the progress and degree of compliance with policy directives. Third, incentives in the form of rewards or sanctions must be available to induce compliance or, fourth, there must be sufficient authority to obtain compliance without resorting to incentives.

Each of these factors in practice turned out to be problematic. Federal action programs in education were motivated by a host of stated and unstated goals, many of them social and political in nature that had little to do with the programs' educational content. Indeed, the coalition of both congressmen and constituent interest groups that was put together to assure passage of the enabling legislation was broad enough to ensure a diversity of goals, many of them conflicting. In order to avoid confronting these differences, it was necessary to couch the program in language that was frequently ambiguous and vague.

As for mutual knowledge, little is known about the learning process itself, let alone how best to provide so-called compensatory education. That program guidelines are often vague, ambiguous, self-contradictory, and unfathomable not only makes it impossible for even a conscientious local school administrator to know precisely how to comply, but also prevents federal project managers and evaluators from knowing whether local districts have complied. Apparently, money is the major incentive at the federal government's command, but its impact depends on both the existence of effective authority to monitor local activities and the ability to withdraw funds for noncompliance. For a variety of reasons, neither condition could be met.

Meanwhile, developments within the federal bureaucracy itself produced a pattern of instability in federal programming that further diminished the ability and the inclination of local school people to comply with federal programs. The dramatic increase in federal activity in education during the 1960s brought a flood of new personnel into the Office of Education. The political origins of the new programs and their large funding gave them high visibility, thereby magnifying the political stakes attached to them. Together these conditions created an atmosphere in which the federal bureaucrats had a strong self-interest in becoming identified with "new innovative" programs in order to advance their careers. Old programs were dropped so that new ones could be publicized, and constant internal struggles were waged to gain power and control over resources and to ensure that programs and jobs would be redefined and relabeled.

Furthermore, after 1968 the Nixon administration's efforts to centralize power in the White House effectively curtailed OE's ability to make policy decisions. The White House, in turn, was both reluctant to make its own decisions regarding education and unwilling to enforce whatever policy directives it did make. This lack of support and absence of follow-through from top executive policymakers added to the unstable and erratic quality of educational policy.

In the general disorder, lower echelon bureaucrats were perhaps most in control of policy administration. For while the Office of Management and Budget, the secretary of HEW, and the commissioner of education may approve some general policies, a career civil servant negotiates specific grants. Accustomed to the swirl of shifting power alliances and policies within government, federal civil servants are unimpressed by rapid changes in executive priorities, cautious in their own movements, and ambivalent about seeking change in educational practices. Their "good working relationships" with state and local colleagues are well established and stable, and they are reluctant to unsettle these relationships by enforcing regulations that may not be clear or that might soon be altered.

The short step from executive policymakers who plan federal programs to career civil servants who administer them can have a critical effect on whether and how much of the original intent gets passed along. The distance between the Office of Education and the classroom is of course much greater than that first step. In fact, a program must pass through three different bureaucratic and political systems—federal, state, and local—each one a congeries of conflicting interests and values. When the program in question seeks educational change, individuals and structures at every level must themselves undergo change. Viewed this way, implementation of federal change programs becomes an awesome task. Furthermore, the top-down delivery mechanism on which federal programs depend cannot work in the absence of effective incentives or sanctions for ensuring compliance. Federal administrators either lack these necessary weapons or are unwilling to use them.

Although some federal programs have sought to bypass state education agencies (SEAs) to work directly with local education agencies (LEAs), SEAs have continued to play a critical role. Federal officials still view SEAs as the primary reference group, both because of the long traditions of working together and because states are constitutionally responsible for providing education.

When federal aid to education increased with the passage of ESEA, SEAs figured prominently as beneficiaries. Providing large grants to SEAs not only assured their support in passing the legislation but also aimed at improving their capacity to carry out federal programs. Categorical grants to SEAs also gave federal planners an opportunity to assert their priorities at the state level; the grants not only financed the growth of SEAs but also tried to influence the direction of that growth. Although OE became the dominant force behind the growth and reorientation of SEAs, it nonetheless had only limited success in winning SEA compliance, due largely, once again, to its inability or unwillingness to exert its authority. This strategically weak bargaining position has led OE to defer to states' prerogatives.

In the search for explanations at the local level for the failure of federal efforts to change school practice, numerous studies have focused on the nature and the cause of the schools' apparent conservatism and organizational rigidity. Factors such as the multiplicity and diffuseness of educational goals, the difficulty in measuring educational outcomes, the power and insulation of professionalism, limitations on lay scrutiny and involvement, organizational fragmentation, an internal culture of conservatism and individualism, and the absence of competition or of sanctions for failure have been identified and analyzed as school-based impediments to change.

Although these factors no doubt operate at the local level, there is a need to recognize the role of local self-interest in determining schools' receptivity to federal change programs. Federal planners, assuming that local schools would share their goals for educational improvement, concentrated on perfecting the programs themselves so that schools would have only to implement them. In pursuing this "rational" approach, however, they failed to anticipate how their efforts would be interpreted from the local perspective.

Local school administrators often see the influx of federal funds as a temporary windfall. The innovative programs these funds pay for are too expensive to be supported by tight local budgets, and the government's record of replacing old programs with new ones every few years makes it extremely risky to institute these programs on a permanent basis. To local administrators, the rational thing to do is often to divert the federal money to existing items in their own budget.

Most of the attempts to explain the failure of federal change programs in education have concentrated on the barriers these programs encountered at the various bureaucratic and intergovernmental levels. Left relatively unexamined was the strategy for change itself, a strategy dependent on the efficacy of top-down policy directives and of technological approaches to change borrowed from industry and the military. The same top-down and technological biases were even more salient in the federal government's involvement with educational research and development, a role that burgeoned simultaneously and in parallel fashion with the growth in its funded programs.

The Federal Role in Research and Development

The federal government's entry into the field of educational research and development (R&D) was a momentous event. The major policy goal was to assert the primacy of federal priorities in a massive attempt to improve education, which was treated as a central national goal. With high expectations that R&D would prove as successful in education as it already had in industry and the military, a strategy was adopted based on a technological or engineering model of change.

Prior to 1965, OE had supported the research projects of scholars who proposed their unsolicited projects to the Cooperative Research Program (CRP), set up in 1956 to screen such proposals. When CRP funds jumped from $15.8 million in 1965 to $49.8 million in 1966, several modifications in policy took place that triggered significant long-range trends in the ways R&D was supported and pursued. One of these was a gradual shift from support for the traditional project research to the targeting of problem areas and consequently increased funding for "procured research." Under this system, the agency that will fund the research virtually writes the proposal in a Request for Proposal (RFP), and applicants then bid for the contract to do the specified work. The object is to ensure that research funds are concentrated in areas of high federal priority. Furthermore, by writing detailed specifications into RFPs, the funding agency gains commensurate control over the conduct of the research. An anomalous situation ensues in which the federal government becomes both the sponsor and the client of the contracted work, an arrangement that effectively gives the funding agency monopoly control.

By 1970, OE was conspicuous among the complex of agencies composing HEW for its unusually large investment in development. In fact, OE's proportional allocations that year for basic research, applied research, and development more closely resembled those of the Department of Defense (DOD) than those of HEW, figures that significantly reflect the change model being applied to education.

Agency	Basic Research	Applied Research	Development
HEW	28%	62%	10%
OE	8%	31%	61%
DOD	3%	15%	81%

Perhaps the most tangible contribution of the R&D boom of the 1960s was the creation of research and development centers and regional educational laboratories under Title IV of ESEA. Designed to bridge the chasm between basic and applied research and program development and dissemination, these new institutions, it was hoped, would reduce the often cited interval of thirty to fifty years between the discovery of knowledge and its application in educational practice. The university-based R&D centers would concentrate on research applied to targeted problem areas and development of programs incorporating new knowledge, and the "autonomous" regional laboratories on developing, demonstrating, and disseminating new programs and products, that is, translating research findings into practice.

Establishment of the centers and the laboratories must also be viewed, however, as another step in consolidating federal control over the content and the execution of educational R&D, even though the regional laboratories theoretically were supposed to adjust to local differences, and structurally they were supposedly independent of OE. For despite their decentralized aspect, they could not fail to be sensitive to their dependency on their creator, chief client, and benefactor. Instead of attending to regional contexts, in fact, or perceiving local people as clients, the laboratories were obliged to respond to national goals as defined by the Office of Education. Central control was enforced by tight supervision and uniform annual budget procedures, and laboratories that did not conform faced a cutoff of their funding. Indeed, some laboratories spent half their resources just in maintaining liaison with OE.

It is widely acknowledged that federally supported R&D has had little impact on schools. Of various explanations offered for this failure to translate new knowledge into practice, some focus on conditions of federal management, such as internal political struggles that resulted in constant turnover in leadership affecting R&D, or a discontinuity in programs related to social and political pressures for new programs, including a propensity for faddism. Other explanations cite factors at the delivery level, especially local recalcitrance and resistance to new ideas and practices. This perspective has spawned a substantial interest in the problem of implementation, one that assumes the existence of a proven innovation and explores strategies for inducing practitioners to accept it. Such explanations, however, overlook the two most fundamental characteristics of the federal role in promoting educational change, whether in its sponsorship of local programs or in its support for educational R&D: its policy of asserting central priorities and its strategy of applying a technological model of change. Both are inappropriate for education as well as self-defeating in their misapprehension of how change takes place.

The Federal Change Model

The first major educational change effort to receive large-scale federal support was the curriculum reform movement of the late 1950s and early 1960s. Fueled by the shock of the Soviet Sputnik achievement, this early movement set patterns for approaches to change that have persisted to this day, including the pursuit of central national goals in educational change, a predisposition toward technological solutions, a belief that an innovation that works in one setting can be spread to many others, an assumption that teachers will passively adopt externally devised innovations, and a generally inadequate and inaccurate understanding of how change takes place. Only in recent years have some of these holdovers from the curriculum reform movement been seriously questioned.

Some of the most decisive lapses that led to the failure of the curriculum reform movement occurred because the reformers were university scholars who had little contact with public schools and tended to ignore the realities of classroom and school organization. Mistaking development and delivery of an innovation for its implementation, they failed to place sufficient emphasis on the process of change, which is determined by the culture of the school, its social and psychological dimensions, and the roles and relationships of individuals within the school organization.

In education, the R&D boom that began in the early 1960s was directed at producing change by generating and disseminating innovations. The first coherent, explicit conceptual model of educational change that emerged from this boom became known as the research, development, and diffusion (RD&D) paradigm. A product of the confident liberalism of the Kennedy era, it reflected a belief that research and the proper application of new knowledge could solve technical, societal, and indeed any problems that might be encountered. It was primarily a matter of attention, application, and money—of engineering. Embodying this engineering approach, the RD&D paradigm soon became the dominant way of conceptualizing the creation and implementation of change.

The RD&D paradigm was based on a conception of educational research as a linear progression from basic scientific investigation through program development and field testing to demonstration and dissemination. The reason for the failure of the process to bring about changes in practice, it was believed, lay toward the research end of the sequence. If practitioners had failed to implement changes deemed desirable by research, it was because the research was not sufficiently product-oriented, and existing programs were wholly inadequate for translating and transmitting research findings for use by practitioners.

Two key assumptions underlay this conception of the research-to-implementation process: first, that innovations originate in research and must be turned into finished products before they reach practitioners; second, that practitioners play a relatively passive role in dissemination and implementation.

With the planning in this model concentrated at the research end, and directed chiefly by government officials, the practitioner is given no function except to accept or reject the finished product. However, a teacher who weighs the consequences of changing or maintaining behavior in the well-established social system of the school is not likely to see much in common with the goals of the planner.

The RD&D paradigm is a top-down strategy, with power and control concentrated at the planning level, and with a hierarchical division of labor. Practitioners are accorded the least power of all in this formula and are expected to be passive at best, resistant at worst. But this overlooks the fact that practitioners are in the position of ultimate power, since the entire process culminates in their decision to accept or reject the product. There are two conditions under which such a scheme of top-down direction and division of labor could work. One is goals and values shared among participants at the different stages or levels; that is, all have a common interest in seeing the products diffused and implemented. This condition does not exist. The other condition is power to force compliance with central directives. But local school people belong to a system of great local autonomy, and their willing cooperation is necessary to induce any substantial change. In addition, once they close their classroom doors, teachers are beyond the power of almost anyone.

Another criticism of the RD&D model focuses on its implicit faith in universal solutions. It assumes that experts can create, produce, and package innovations that will be widely applicable. Such an assumption theoretically justifies the huge initial cost at the development stage with savings at the distribution end through wide dissemination of a proven product. This belief in the ability to find generalizable solutions in the form of innovations that will transfer from one setting to another, known as the "doctrine of transferability," is part of the creed of an industrialized, technocratic society that places great faith in the ability of experts to "fix" social problems. Success in meeting material needs through technical means is assumed to be applicable to social problems as well.

In common with earlier curriculum reformers, the RD&D model, by assuming that "proven" innovations will be readily adopted by practitioners, ignores the complexity of schools as social systems. By giving little attention to the nature of the "user system" the model not only naively assumes a willingness to adopt packaged innovations but also underestimates the difficulties in learning new materials and practices. It also ignores the diversity of educational objectives.

Despite a growing body of evidence that local factors tend to overwhelm imported innovations, that practitioners will more readily resist than adopt programs not of their own making, and that delivering an innovation does not guarantee that it will be implemented as intended, many of the concepts and assumptions at work in the RD&D paradigm continue to influence reformers, particularly national government planners. These ideas survive because they serve needs peculiarly suited to a federal role in education: pursuit of central goals and assertion of federal priorities; bureaucratic control over the process; and economic values such as economy of scale, efficiency, marketability, and productivity. Perspectives on educational change, however, have been modified by the experiences of the past two decades.

Shifts in Federal Policy

Ever since the curriculum reform movement of the 1950s, the evolution of theories and models of change in education has been marked by several generally consistent trends. One of these has been a shift "downward" in the focal point of change. The early assumption that innovations and the impetus for change must come from the top of the educational hierarchy and filter down to the practitioner was followed by the now generally accepted principle that the key to successful change is found at the local level. A related trend has been from an early, almost exclusive emphasis on the innovation itself to the current primary concern for the process of innovation. While most attention, in keeping with the engineering model and the doctrine of transferability, once focused on generating "proven" innovations on the assumption that receptive practitioners would automatically adopt them, today the main issues are implementation and improving practitioners' capacity to change.

Both of these trends signal a new respect for the role and power of the practitioner. A good deal of this respect was accorded as a result of the so-called change agent studies carried out for OE by the Rand Corporation. Called "one of the most extensive examinations of the change process in recent time," the Rand research studied nearly three hundred projects under various federal programs supporting educational change. Perhaps its most critical finding was that implementation was essentially an organizational process characterized by "mutual adaptation." In other words, when a planned project confronts the organizational setting that it is intended to occupy and change, concessions on both sides are necessary to implement it successfully. In addition to changes expected from practitioners adopting a project, the designed project itself must change to accommodate the practitioners in their unique organizational settings. Projects that were not flexible enough to permit this accommodation tended not to survive the implementation process.

It is not overstating the case to say that the practitioner has won a political victory in gaining recognition as a powerful and legitimate force to be reckoned with. This victory has caused a reexamination of the fundamental assumptions underlying the repeated failures of unilateral attempts to introduce change. In a mood that might be called "the new modesty," change theorists have been forced to reevaluate the engineering model, which relies on finding the "most effective" solution to a given educational problem; the doctrine of transferability, according to which innovations that work under one set of circumstances can be made to work elsewhere; and the power of central sponsors or authorities to make change happen as an intended outcome of the policy process.

The new knowledge certainly seems calculated to induce modesty: there are no proven solutions, or at least they have not been found; even if there were, they would probably not transfer; and even if they did, the practitioners would probably reject them. This has caused no little consternation over what is seen as a paradox facing policymakers. On the one hand, as Dale Mann of Teachers College, Columbia University, has observed:

Change is whatever the service deliverers—schools and teachers—decide it is to be. The less self-determination is allowed to these ultimate implementers of change, the less total change will result. On the other hand, the Federal government has a responsibility to cause improvements in education. We expect the Federal government to make change happen even where local authorities—including teachers—may disagree. The decisions of local level actors about what changes should or should not be implemented are legitimate decisions. But so are the decisions of Federal level administrators. If the delivery level autonomy must be maximized for there to be any change, yet that autonomy vitiates or contradicts Federal decisions, and if both sets of actors are making good faith, legitimate decisions, then how can there be a user-driven Federally supported system of school improvement?[2]

The onset of the new modesty occurred during a Republican administration that sought to pull back from programmatic initiatives in most areas of social policy. With seeemingly ample justification provided by the record of failed change attempts, the Nixon administration called for better knowledge as a prerequisite to new programs, and the National Institute of Education (NIE) was established in 1972 to provide it. Much of the theorizing that took place during this time revolved around reducing the gap between R&D and school practice, both to make R&D more user-oriented and "relevant" and to give practitioners a greater role in determining what they wanted from R&D. Both of these concerns involved gaining greater knowledge of the schools and their personnel.

In 1973, NIE issued a major report outlining its evolving policy toward educational change. It stated that the past practice of contracting with R&D organizations to carry out work on targeted, nationally defined problems had created a burgeoning system of institutions external to the schools and poorly coordinated with them. A de facto decision had been made not to support development of local school system R&D capacity. Reviewing past R&D practice, the report also criticized the predominant linear model of change that places practitioners at the receiving end as passive consumers of R&D products. In a major reformulation of policy, the NIE report proposed both to close the gap between R&D and school practice and to build a problem-solving capacity into the operating system.

The report did not propose, however, to reduce the role either of R&D or of the federal government. It observed that schools lacked the capacity to effect their own renewal and needed help. It also cited the need to know more about what works in a given setting and about the complexity of the setting itself. Both these conditions, according to the report, served to enlarge the task of R&D, whose purpose is to produce generalizable knowledge and materials. Indeed, the recommendations that concluded the report seemed intended to support the extant R&D system at least as much as to accomplish the objective of building local capacities for self-improvement. All the recommendations served to strengthen the ties among researchers, developers, and practitioners without

[2] Dale Mann, "The User-Driven System and a Modest Proposal," *Teachers College Record* 79 (February 1978): 389.

shifting any initiatory power from the planners to the practitioners. The total innovation process would still be controlled by the federal government.

NIE's most recent official statement in this area has been its policy on instructional program improvement, issued in March of 1977. The new policy reflects a self-described "critical reexamination of the Institute's priorities" that has been occasioned by the new national administration, including the appointment of a new NIE director and other top level staff, and by the need to face a number of pressing criticisms surrounding the past two decades of federal investment in curriculum reform. The direction this reappraisal would take had already been previewed in a substantial decline in the proportion of NIE's budget assigned to development activities, from 72 percent of the total budget in FY 1975, to 58 percent in FY 1976, and to 43 percent in FY 1977. According to NIE, this decline reflects both the scheduled completion of a number of expensive development projects inherited from the regional laboratories and the R&D centers and the institute's decision not to initiate much new full-scale development.

The new policy, issued by NIE's policy-setting National Council on Educational Research, established priorities among the institute's possible roles in promoting educational change. In order of priority, they are: applied research; efforts to strengthen others' development capabilities; "prototypic development" of new instructional programs; and "full-scale development" of new instructional programs. NIE sees itself constrained by these priorities to support the strengthening of the educational system's own curriculum development capabilities in ways that are least directive, while itself becoming the agency of last resort in the production and distribution of instructional materials. There will be more money made available for grants and less reliance on procured R&D through requests for proposals.

The new modesty with regard to the ability of central planners and developers to initiate change in local schools has found expression in NIE's new policy, as evidenced by the withdrawal from development activities, the emphasis on research, and the purported retreat from directiveness. The difficulty of truly departing from past assumptions and practice suggests that a healthy skepticism toward this new policy is appropriate. It is hard to predict, for example, to what extent federal control will actually diminish under the new policy or how active practitioners will become as developers of their own programs. Though deemphasized, the continued faith in both prototypic and full-scale development evokes shades of the engineering model. The doctrine of transferability has survived. Such reservations notwithstanding, NIE's self-proclaimed moratorium on its sponsorship of large-scale, centralized curriculum development in favor of better knowledge and more self-sufficiency for the user system should not be underestimated.

Conclusion

Strategists of educational change now have two substantial and growing bases of knowledge to help in future planning: experience with past federally sponsored attempts at change and new research on implementation of innovative programs at the practitioner level. If the experience has not been happy from the standpoint of desired change in school practice, it has, to say the least, been instructive. In the welter of lessons to be learned, three may be singled out. First, political factors intrude in direct proportion to the length of the line between the planner and the practitioner. The greater this distance, the more likely is the change agenda to be distorted by competing political demands. Second, political interference also varies directly with the scale of a change program. Large-scale reform programs multiply the political interests at stake, creating complexities that have proven intractable. Third, whatever political factors may impinge on imported or large-scale programs, practitioners have shown that they have the power to reject programs to which they are not committed. Reformers have been forced to focus on the practitioner and the process of implementation.

The growing body of research on the practitioner has begun to shed some light on the reality of schools as social systems, the awesome complexity of which has been so consistently underestimated in past strategies. Among the findings that emerge most clearly are the primacy of personal contact and the necessity for practitioners to participate in program development. Effective implementation requires personal interaction and contacts among practitioners and between practitioners and planners if the painstaking process of changing old roles and learning new ones is to occur. This close personal contact is notably absent from most change efforts.

As for participation, the need for those who are expected to implement a new program to take an active part in the innovative process—such as planning, designing, problem-solving, and decision-making—has become virtually an article of faith for effective implementation. Dale Mann's suggestion that policy-makers "let a thousand wheels be reinvented" recognized the importance to a practitioner of developing one's own innovative answer to an immediately felt problem. That experts somewhere else have already pondered a similar problem in the abstract and labored to produce potentially an equally effective solution could not matter less to practitioners. Against the protests of cost-effectiveness people, Dale Mann poses the following rhetorical question: Which is preferable, that school people go through the horribly inefficient process of rediscovering the usefulness of an axle stuck through a disc, or a situation in which heaps of wheels lie around unused because of the local conviction that "they won't work here"?[3]

The developing knowledge indicates that federal planners will have to reconcile federal purposes and programs regarding school change with slowness, smallness, diversity, little central control, and great expense. As one study recently concluded, these conditions "may not be politically and financially feasible

---

[3] Ibid., 405.

in many situations, but there is no question that effective implementation will not occur without them."[4]

Federal planners have no reason to be pleased with their past efforts to effect educational change, but they have learned much from their failure. It remains to be seen, however, whether they will apply what they have learned to the development of future programs.

[4] Michael Fullan and Alan Pomfret, "Research on Curriculum and Instruction Implementation," *Review of Educational Research* 47 (Winter 1977): 335–97.

Grateful acknowledgement is given to Constancia Warren for her helpful suggestions in preparing this essay.

Federal Policies
and Private Schools

THOMAS VITULLO-MARTIN

Federal aid to private elementary and secondary schools preceded aid to public schools. The first example of direct federal aid to a school appears to have occurred in 1810, when Thomas Jefferson arranged for the Departments of Interior and War to provide the rent for a Catholic schoolhouse in Detroit. For almost two hundred years, the federal government has aided private schools, and, as its role in American political life has grown, the characteristics of the policies that aid private schools have changed. Federal aid policies follow four patterns, loosely related to stages of growth in the importance of federal policies. No sharp divisions in the chronological successions stand out, however, and some first-stage policies can be found in current legislation.

First, the federal government made direct grants or endowment contributions to specific schools, public or private, to obtain their general education services. These grants ensured that schools would be available for children under federal jurisdiction and evidently involved virtually no federal direction of the content of the education. Then, the government began to underwrite or offer other inducements to schools, public or private, that supplied federally desired programs. Next, the federal government expanded this concept to include all programs that schools normally offer—in other words, it proposed a type of general education aid that would include private schools. (Most general aid approaches have been subsequently blocked by the current interpretation of the First Amendment.) Finally, the federal government has turned to a formula whereby it provides services to private school students without providing resources that can be used by the school. It funds public school systems to serve private school students. This awkward arrangement, which substantially affects the relations between public and private schools, was adopted to satisfy constitutional interpretations that require, in effect, that the state and private schools keep their distance from each other.

The discussion of types of aid turns naturally to a discussion of regulation, for as the federal government has gradually become more specific in identifying precisely the kinds of changes it wishes to make in local public and private education, and which groups it targets its aid to reach, aid bills have become increasingly regulative in their effects. Finally, federal policies are emerging with purely regulative effects on private schools—regulations unalloyed with aid. The most recent and significant of these regulations are in the Internal Revenue Code. The introduction of the tax code into a discussion of federal education policies may seem surprising. But no comprehensive review of federal aid to education can be restricted to the programs of the Office of Education (OE).

Federal aid or regulations affecting private schools have been administered by a surprising number of federal departments, including Army, Navy, Defense, Interior, Labor, Housing and Urban Development, Treasury, and Health, Education, and Welfare, and by offices such as the Veterans Administration, Social Security Administration, Bureau of Indian Affairs, Office of Education, and National Institute of Mental Health.

Patterns of Aid

The federal government began aiding schools because it needed education services in areas over which it had primary jurisdiction. At first, its grants and similar aids made little distinction between private and public schools. It purchased services from whatever kind of schools that would provide them.

The first congressional actions aiding private and public education immediately followed the conclusion of the Revolutionary War. The 1783 Treaty of Paris ceded the Northwest Territory to the Congress of the Confederation. Congress took direct responsibility for governing the Northwest Territory. In the Northwest Ordinance of 1787, which set out the procedure for governing the territory and for dividing it into self-governing states, the Congress of the Confederation made clear that its scheme of aid was intended to benefit religious schools: "Religion, morality and knowledge being necessary to good government and the happiness of mankind, schools and the means of education shall forever be encouraged."

The territorial legislature was to select the sections of land to be given to the territories for education and the schools it would serve, subject to the approval of Congress. A number of Catholic schools that were open to all students were supported under provisions of the ordinance. With time, the territories became states, and Congress was no longer responsible for the provision of basic elementary and secondary education. But even today Congress has not completely divested itself of responsibility for education in certain specific areas. It has jurisdiction over Indian reservations, where Congress has a treaty obligation to provide education; military bases and reservations, where the established federal practice is to provide for the educational needs of the armed forces and their dependents; and the District of Columbia, the Panama Canal Zone, the Commonwealth of Puerto Rico, the Virgin Islands, Samoa, and the Pacific Trust Territory. In each of these types of jurisdiction, Congress provides funds for the operating subsidies to specific private schools. In several instances,

√

Congress provides direct grants to private schools or provides indirect subsidies, either through grants to local legislatures, which in turn support private schools, or through tuition payments for federally dependent residents enrolled in private schools.

The Morrill Act of 1862 was the first federal program to alter educational policies within the existing states by funding specific and limited types of educational services that in some instances had been provided by the states. Administered by the Department of Agriculture, it set aside public lands within each state for the endowment of agricultural colleges, which could be under private auspices. The program was enlarged, and direct federal appropriations have been provided since the Second Morrill Act was passed in 1890.

In 1917, Congress applied the same broad categorical concept to schools below the college level with the Smith-Hughes Act, administered by the Department of Labor, which gave vocational education grants to the states to train teachers and establish programs. The Smith-Hughes Act required that the program be under public supervision or control, and this clause was generally interpreted to exclude private schools, but the states were given substantial responsibility for administering the act, and some may have included private schools in their programs.

In 1968, the Vocational Education Act, which succeeded the Smith-Hughes Act, was amended to provide vocational education service to private school students, following the child-benefit formula devised for the Elementary and Secondary Education Act of 1965 (ESEA). In 1974 Congress again amended the act. Section 122(a)(7) provides "vocational training through arrangements with private vocational training institutions where such private institutions can make a significant contribution to attaining the objectives of the state plan, and can provide substantially equivalent training at lesser cost, or can provide equipment or services not available in public institutions. . . ." Of all federal laws, this provision of support for private institutions' operating costs related to vocational education comes closest to general education aid to private schools. It is, however, quite clearly directed at a specific education program, though a broad one.

The federal approach to vocational education has also been applied to the education of handicapped persons. Beginning in 1963, the Mental Retardation Facilities Construction Act and the Community Mental Health Centers Act authorized grants by the National Institute of Mental Health of up to 75 percent of total costs for the construction of facilities for training teachers to educate the handicapped and for operating special education programs. Private, nonprofit schools were eligible. Also in 1963, Congress substantially increased the funding of Title V of the Social Security Act, which provides the federal share of operating expenses for these institutions. Substantial portions of the operating costs of the participating private institutions are public funds. The Education for All Handicapped Children Act of 1975 greatly expanded its provisions and made private institutions equally eligible with public ones.

In 1977, the act was amended to incorporate the idea of mainstreaming, that is, placing handicapped students in regular classrooms, and to guarantee "free and public" education to all handicapped children. Through mainstreaming, public school systems will be able to capture the substantially higher amounts of public money available for the education of the handicapped, an incentive for them to pursue the program energetically. Private institutions have greater difficulty mainstreaming because the public funding of students mainstreamed in private schools appears to raise complex legal and constitutional questions. Furthermore, the act's requirement of "free and public" education could mean that public institutions may displace private ones, especially as funding levels increase.

Beginning in 1945, hearings were held on bills to provide across-the-board assistance to the poorer states to raise their per pupil expenditure to a basic minimum. In 1946 a bill reported, but not voted on, by the Senate would have provided a subsidy guaranteeing a per pupil expenditure of $55 in each state. The bill included private school children in those states aiding private schools, but opposition to the measure from groups opposed to aid for religious schools mounted. In 1948, the bill passed the Senate by a vote of 58-22, but was blocked in the House. In 1949, conflict over the religious issue became acute, and both the House and the Senate refused to vote on the bill. Many states at that time provided aid to private schools in one form or another, and the law would have permitted them to continue their local practices. Today fourteen states provide aid to private schools or to their students, including states that pay private school tuition, and thirty-three states offer at least some child-welfare benefits to private school children, such as school transportation.

The attempt to fund private schools through grants to the states, following state laws, would have solved a number of the most difficult political problems surrounding the private aid issue, but it is an idea whose time has passed. Some existing federal grant programs do permit the states to establish their own positions on aiding private schools, such as the program for the handicapped already mentioned, in which state offices of education may or may not contract with private schools to provide handicapped students with education services, but it is not likely to be an important approach in future federal legislation.

Federal aid-to-education programs that include private school students have received the greatest political acceptance when they have been directed at meeting some specific national need. The school lunch program and the school milk program of 1946 and 1954, administered by the Department of Agriculture, subsidized both public and private school students and were not found politically objectionable—despite the heat generated at the time by the issue of general aid to private schools. Both of these programs gave resources and control to private schools and paid them to administer the program. The school lunch and school milk programs originated in the agricultural committees of Congress and were designed to benefit farmers and dairymen. In such cases, proposed legislation to include private schools in aid programs mobilizes interest groups outside education, and the public-private school issue may be swept aside.

In 1958, the National Defense Education Act (NDEA) included special low-interest, long-term loans to private schools for the purchase of science-related equipment. The same legislation provided outright grants to public schools for construction and equipment costs. Initially, NDEA aided private schools more equitably in theory than in practice. By the end of the first three years, 85 percent of the authorized grants for public schools had been allocated to them, but only 8 percent of the loans available to private schools had been committed.

Title VII of NDEA also permitted private schools to receive contracts for education research and demonstration programs that met national defense education objectives. Private schools may apply for education research projects under NDEA and other funding programs, although under current law they would be ineligible to receive funds to carry on any programs they pioneered once the programs are proven effective and ready for diffusion.

NDEA seems to have succeeded in including private schools because its goal was to improve national defense by stimulating the development of science. Thus Congress's purpose overrode the institutional rivalry between public and private schools. The bill's focus on hardware, rather than operating expenses of science education, may also have quieted opposition.

NDEA also directly subsidized the salaries of private school teachers and provided them with a number of indirect subsidies, such as summer training institutes in languages and science. The 1964 amendments extended the cancellation feature of the NDEA Title II loans to private school teachers, who had previously been excluded. Under the current cancellation clause, 10 percent of the principal of an NDEA loan (now called a National Direct Student Loan) is canceled each year for five years if the loan recipient is teaching in certain types of schools. The clause is a valuable salary subsidy, especially to a beginning teacher, since it saves the borrower "after tax" dollars and also delays payback for a five-year, interest-free period. Also, the NDEA amendments of 1964 gave private school teachers attending summer institutes the same stipends paid to public school teachers.

By excluding private schools in the initial legislation, NDEA placed them at a disadvantage in the competition with public schools for teachers. As federal intervention in education increases in magnitude, this problem will become more acute. Some federal programs, either alone or in conjunction with state programs, have subsidized public school budgets specifically to increase the level of teacher expertise to meet particularly difficult educational problems. Since private schools cannot directly receive federal aid for teachers' salaries, although the salaries can themselves be indirectly subsidized, the federal program sets them at a competitive disadvantage. For example, the Bilingual Education Act of 1974 makes grants to public school districts to support bilingual programs, which may include salaries for bilingual education specialists. The program makes it profitable for the public schools to pay a premium for teachers with bilingual skills. Although private school students are to be included in the programs offered by the public schools, this is practically impossible under most program designs, since the bilingual instruction often takes place simultaneously with instruction in reading, mathematics, social studies, and similar subjects. Private schools with bilingual programs generally serve low-income families, have low per pupil revenues, and survive by economizing in a number of ways, including paying teachers low salaries. Their public school competitors in several cities have hired away their bilingual teachers after winning federal grants, forcing some private schools to terminate their programs.

Title I of the Elementary and Secondary Education Act of 1965 (ESEA) introduced a new approach. Previous programs—school lunch and NDEA, for example—benefited private school students by placing resources under the control of the private institutions. By the time ESEA was considered, for all practical purposes the Supreme Court had prevented Congress from continuing that approach in any basic education aid programs. But Congress was unwilling to pass school aid legislation that did not include private school students.

Congress adopted a "child-benefit" approach, establishing broad criteria for identifying children in need of special education services. It provided funds to public school systems for diagnosing the student's learning problems and supplying the needed educational services. The program left local school districts with discretion over the criteria used to identify eligible students, the approach to diagnosing the problems, and the kinds of services, staffing, and evaluation they would provide. A student's enrollment in public or private schools was not to be a factor in his selection for Title I services.

The child-benefit approach received particular support from the heavily Democratic Northeast and Midwest—where private school student populations are large—because legislators realized that the inclusion of private school students would substantially increase the total amount of aid their regions would receive. Aid would be distributed to public schools according to the area's population, not public school enrollment. As a result, the ESEA aid bill has become the principal legislation by which the federal government directly regulates public and private school relationships.

The Emergency School Assistance Program (ESAP) and the Emergency School Aid Act of 1972 (ESAA), which provided funds for programs that would further integration or relieve the problems of segregation, followed the pattern of ESEA. Education services would be provided to private school children by public school employees, as part of the public school program, and the approach has been routinely followed in subsequent legislation. Congress has also funded public schools to attend to the needs of eligible students in private schools in several other social and educational programs. In addition to federal education programs, funds from other programs have been applied to the needs of private school students in some communities. The Community Development (CD) Block Grant program, for example, funds scholarships to private schools for residents of CD target areas in some communities. CD funds have gone directly to private schools to provide residents of target areas with remedial services and to rehabilitate school buildings. Funds from the Comprehensive Employment and Training Act (CETA) program have also been granted to some private schools sponsoring CETA job-training programs. These activities continue a long tradition of involving private schools in federal economic development programs.

Patterns of Regulation

Almost all federal aid programs regulate their recipients, but the degree of regulation varies greatly. All education aid programs entail a kind of contract between the federal government and the state, the local school district, or the private school. The recipient, in turn, is to spend that money for some specified service the federal government wishes to support. If the service is not provided in the specified manner, the aid ceases.

The degree of regulation depends on the degree of specificity about the recipient's duties and the extent of enforcement in the contract or grant. Some contracts do not go into detail. General school aid bills discussed in the 1940s through the early 1960s, for example, would have required little from the states in order for them to comply with the contract terms; they would simply have had to spend the money on education. Under the child-benefit approach, Congress turned to categorical aid programs, specifying who would be served, what kinds of services or materials would be provided, and under what conditions. Thus, although categorical grants were voluntary school aid programs—which states, local districts, and private schools had to apply for if they wished to receive grants—these categorical programs nevertheless often became highly regulated ones.

The federal government has regulated private education since the early nineteenth century. Through the Supreme Court's power of constitutional review of state legislation, it began by regulating the conduct of the states toward private schools. Later the federal government began direct regulation of private schools through a number of federal regulatory agencies. More recently, it has been indirectly regulating private schools through categorical aid programs.

The Supreme Court has generally restricted the state's regulation of private education and limited public aid to private schools. But the early cases involving federal aid supported such aid. The Court upheld the commissioner of Indian affairs in providing funds to the Bureau of Catholic Indian Missions in *Quick Bear* v. *Leupp* (1908), and it upheld the provision of textbooks to private school pupils through state funds in *Cochran* v. *Louisiana* (1930). In *Everson* v. *Board of Education of Ewing Township* (1947), the Court held it constitutional to reimburse parents of religious school pupils for busing their children to school and to establish rules for the busing.

In the 1960s and 1970s, the Court considered a number of state laws that sought to subsidize private schools directly, fund programs with specific educational objectives, subsidize tuition payments to private schools, and alter the taxation policies affecting tuition payments. It has not established a principle by which one could predict the judicial outcome of a challenge to state aid laws. The most recent cases appear to have been decided by a bargaining process among the justices. States can pay for school bus transportation to and from private schools but not for field trips in the same buses. States can provide textbooks but not maps and workbooks, and also diagnostic but not remedial services. In considering state aid to private schools, the Court has created a dual system in which aid to private higher education is treated much less restrictively than aid to elementary and secondary schools. In recent years the Court has tended to treat private elementary and secondary schools as similar to public schools insofar as they are properly subject to the powers of state and federal regulative agencies but to emphasize their separation when considering policies of direct or indirect general or categorical aid.

The U. S. Office of Education (OE) is the most active agency regulating private schools. Its role as regulator has increased in recent years, and it is felt more by some types of private schools than others. Initially, OE regulated only the activities of the recipients that were related to their use of the funds. Thus, in ESEA Title I, at first only the Title I portion of the public school budgets was examined. As the categorical programs have matured the inadequacy of the early federal approach became apparent, and regulations and monitoring were extended to cover many of the nonfederally funded activities. OE, in particular, enlarged regulations designed to ensure that federal programs would not have the effect of segregating pupils and that the districts would not bypass the intent of categorical federal aid by using federal funds to replace local funds.

Only a few private schools are directly affected by federal enforcement of regulations attached to categorical programs, because only a few directly receive funds from federal sources. There are direct federal subsidies to private schools for the handicapped, to certain other private schools at the elementary and secondary level, and to almost all private colleges. These schools are subject to much greater federal regulation than private schools that do not receive federal funds.

Nevertheless, the private elementary and secondary schools whose students receive Title I services provided by public schools do not totally escape the effects of regulation. In order for their children to receive services from the public system, the private schools must submit to the regulations of the public system providing the services. For example, the public school system may require the private school to follow specified program planning procedures in commenting on a Title I proposal. It may require a private school staff to meet state certification requirements in bilingual education before including the private school students in a bilingual program.

Private schools are subject to the direct regulations of a number of other federal agencies, including the National Labor Relations Board, the Environmental Protection Agency, the Occupational Health and Safety Agency, the Equal Employment Opportunity Commission, the Office of Civil Rights, and the Internal Revenue Service (IRS). The IRS is a particularly effective regulator, restricting such activities as political lobbying by private schools or their use of segregationist admissions policies. Violators lose their tax-exempt status. In 1978 the IRS proposed new rules to compel private schools to take positive steps toward integration, such as offering scholarships to minority students, if the schools are not integrated in proportion to the number of minority students in their community. Schools that do not comply will lose their tax-exempt status. The new IRS rules may be amended before final implementation, but they indicate that IRS may assume a much more aggressive regulative posture toward private schools in the future.

The proposed IRS regulations are particularly significant for three reasons. First, they will affect only private schools. Second, the sanctions attached to the regulations—loss of tax-exempt status—would affect the schools' incomes to a greater degree than most court fines, since they would significantly reduce contributions that sustain the schools and may decrease the proceeds from school-operated businesses. Finally, the process by which IRS makes new administrative rules is unfamiliar to most education interest groups, and the legal safeguards that apply in IRS administrative enforcement hearings are more limited than those that apply to most other administrative, civil, and criminal hearings.

Both ESEA and the Internal Revenue Code are examples of the types of laws with important indirect regulative effects on private schools. These laws regulate the behavior of private schools through the rules they establish for third parties, such as public school systems providing federally sponsored education services that include private school students in their programs or families choosing to enroll their children in private schools. For example, federal regulations, at least as interpreted in New York City, prevent public school systems from providing bilingual education services funded under Title VII of ESEA to private school students, unless the private schools provide a state-certified bilingual teacher as the regular classroom teacher. Hence, the law in effect requires the private school to follow the federal regulations or exclude its students from the federal program implemented by the public school system. Strictly considered, however, the law regulates only the public school behavior, preventing it from serving private school students in certain circumstances. Most legislation following the child-benefit approach indirectly regulates private schools, but federal laws outside the education area also have this effect.

Prior to ESEA, public school districts typically gave the politically strongest neighborhoods within their jurisdiction the best school services. In wealthy neighborhoods, one could expect to find the most experienced teachers with the most advanced degrees and the best equipped playground, library, music room, and the like. In the poorest neighborhoods, teachers were inexperienced, classrooms were overcrowded, facilities were minimal, and everything was in need of repair. Per pupil expenditures often varied widely within the same school system. ESEA forced systems to equalize their expenditures among schools, before it would permit the distribution of federal funds.

Title I funds cannot subsidize the regular school program. Title I children must receive special services, over and above those they would ordinarily receive from their school. OE found this aspect of Title I difficult to enforce, for it discovered that many school districts withdrew their own funds and staff from Title I public schools and put them into schools not entitled to receive them. In other words, the districts used the funds as general aid, and Title I provided nothing extra for the eligible students. In the language of Title I, the school districts had "supplanted" local funds with federal funds. The regulation issued to control supplanting simply stated that public school districts had to equalize their per pupil expenditures throughout the schools in a district, at least to the extent that no Title I school received less in local and state funds than ineligible schools on a per pupil basis. Only then could Title I funds be distributed.

ESEA has changed public and private school relationships. Under this legislation, public school districts receive funds in accordance with a formula based only on population and income. The schools then identify eligible students and provide them with services, whether they are in private or public schools. This created problems. Later amendments to ESEA attempted to correct the difficulties by requiring both the formation of parent advisory committees to oversee ESEA programs and by requiring representatives of nonpublic school parents on these committees. They also required that the public system involve private schools early enough in the planning of the ESEA program to ensure that the final proposal reflected the needs of private as well as public school students. Thus the law created a mechanism by which private school representatives—often parents of private school children but also some administrators—could influence public school policy.

The amendments also established a bypass procedure to include private school students in ESEA programs in states whose laws prohibited the state from serving nonpublic school students. Upon an opinion from the state that its constitution or laws prohibit the inclusion of such students in the program, or upon a finding by the commissioner of education that the state or school district does not include these students equitably, the commissioner may remove a proportionate amount of Title I funds from the state's allocation and contract with a private, nonprofit institution to provide them with services. Although the measure is not punitive, it does deprive the public systems of a portion of their staffs and is quite painful to systems using the funds provided by the federal government for private school students to increase the services to public school students. The change forces a cutback in the public school program.

In order for private school students to participate in federally funded programs, the public schools must draft proposals that include them. The quality and suitability of the services the private school students receive depend on the degree to which the private schools have been involved in planning and coordinating programs designed to meet the students' educational needs. In the early years of ESEA and other programs, public schools frequently took no steps to include private school students in their proposals. Often, they failed to consult with the private school administrators to develop the most effective programs for the private school students. The 1974 Education Amendments altered Title VII of ESEA and ESAA by requiring public school systems to provide for the needs of private school students in all grant proposals. The amendments also tightened the requirements that public systems include private schools in the early needs assessment and planning stages that a district applying for Title I funds must complete.

Investigations in 1976 found that state offices of education, which are funded by Congress to administer Title I and other federal education aid programs within their borders, were not monitoring the compliance of local districts required to serve private school children without discrimination. Problems with the amount and quality of the services have persisted, and the 1978 Education Amendments further tightened the regulations. For the first time Congress required equal expenditures, consistent with disability, on students in private and public schools. Congress increased the power of private school representatives to block ESEA grants to districts that do not adequately include private school students and required states to monitor and report on public school systems' compliance with the federal requirement that they include private school students equitably.

The most important federal measures affecting private schools, however, are not education laws but provisions of the Internal Revenue Codes, which restrict the education choices open to parents. In education, they form "an ecology of perverse incentives," in Norton Long's phrase. Three aspects of the tax system affect private education. First, state and local taxes that fund public education expenditures represent deductions from personal and corporate tax liabilities. The deductions disproportionately benefit the wealthy because their tax rates are higher and therefore their dollar tax savings are much greater on the same level of expenditure.

Second, private school tuition expenditures are not tax deductible. Individual private school costs are subject to tax, but public school costs are not. The federal government taxes 10 to 14 percent of the cost of private school tuition through the federal income tax. For families in the highest federal income tax brackets, a before-tax dollar is worth four times an after-tax dollar.

This effect has been aggravated in recent years by the failure of the government to index the tax system, so that the tax rate applying to families paying tuition to private schools has increased without any corresponding improvement in their real ability to pay. Their income and expenses have risen with inflation, and the tax system has increased its rate of taxation. The percentage of income devoted to private education expenses that accrues to the government through the tax system increases each year. The impact of this provision of the tax code has only recently become severe, because only in the 1960s did private religious schools begin, in large numbers, to be financed principally by tuition income. In earlier decades during the period of income taxation, private religious schools were funded principally through tax-deductible contributions to parish churches. The federal income tax revenues from income spent on private education have increased by several hundred percent in the past fifteen years.

Third, the Internal Revenue Codes exempt only certain nonprofit institutions from taxation. These institutions must either meet specific federal regulations or pay taxes. Hence, the penalties for noncompliance are substantial. The federal government has no comparable force to wield over public schools.

Conclusion

A review of federal aid to private schools indicates that Congress has directly aided them in areas that are its direct responsibility. The Supreme Court's ruling of a constitutional limitation on public aid to private education, a recent interpretation, has unreasonably distinguished between elementary and secondary education on the one hand and higher education on the other, and has changed frequently in a contradictory fashion over the past twenty years.

The federal government has aided private (and public) education through a large number of programs housed outside not only the Office of Education but also outside the Department of Health, Education, and Welfare. The child-benefit approach—by which Congress funds public school districts to serve all eligible children, in private as well as in public schools—has been adopted only in HEW programs. Programs outside HEW normally give resources directly to private institutions. Within HEW, OE programs are more stringent in excluding private schools from the control of resources than those in other divisions, such as those operated by the National Institute of Mental Health. The pattern suggests that a traditional interest group politics best explains the development of the federal policies that define private school involvement in federal programs.

Finally, the indirect effects of federal education and taxation policy are responsible for important changes in private education. The child-benefit approach, conceived in part to isolate private schools from federal regulation, has produced greater changes in the organization and behavior of private education, and in the relations of private to public schools, than have all previous federal direct-aid programs combined. Taxation policy, by forcing wealthier parents into suburban public schools at the expense of urban private schools, has substantially increased the degree of segregation experienced by the children of the wealthy, the segregation of residential areas in cities, and the extent of federally subsidized education for the wealthy. Whatever the effects of existing taxation policies, taxation itself is a policy with increasingly regulative effects for private education.

Government in Higher Education

FREDERICK S. LANE

Although universities have always been involved with politics, the current publicness and politicization of higher education in the United States are unprecedented. Here as almost everywhere else in the world the cost of higher education has increasingly been paid by the government, and there is a corresponding claim for accountability for those public funds. There is no facet of American higher education today that is not significantly influenced by government: who attends college, what is studied, which faculty are hired, which public service activities are undertaken, what facilities are constructed, and the quality of instructional and other services delivered.

At the same time that the academic and political worlds interact, a sizable gap widens between the attitudes of academics and politicians toward one another. Academics complain that most politicians have a short-term time perspective. Often there is no continuity to policymaking—programs change from one legislative session to another, each year's committee chairperson moves on to another committee, or pragmatism dictates a quick compromise on issues of great importance. Politicians are primarily concerned with their own narrow constituencies, and they seldom consider the broader public interest. They tend to politicize issues and only view higher education in terms of political benefits and costs. Politicians are often badly informed about higher education and seldom attempt to understand fully the complex issues. As college graduates, or parents of graduates, they often assume unwarranted familiarity with the issues. Finally, they say, politicians are arrogant, enjoy their power, and often demonstrate contempt for those who are not politicians.

Politicians, on the other hand, often hold unfavorable views of academics. They complain that academics do not understand the political process and make politicians' jobs more difficult. Academics, they say, are solely concerned with their own interests, seeking more and more money, seldom have the information needed for policy decisions or the ability to communicate precisely and clearly, and are often arrogant and condescending, paying only lip service to accountability.[1] This clash in perspectives underlies the conflict between the academic community and government officials at the state and federal levels, especially in a period of budgetary austerity and taxpayer revolts.

Higher Education and State Government

In order to compare the current political norms, or conventional attitudes, affecting state higher education policy with those of the past, the four norms discovered by Heinz Eulau and Harold Quinley in their 1968 study for the Carnegie Commission on Higher Education will be discussed. Eulau and Quinley interviewed 102 political leaders, mostly legislators, in nine states. They reported four principal political norms that seemed to govern the politics of higher education in the American states in the post-World War II period and especially in the 1960s (until approximately 1968-69). These norms were low responsiveness, passivity in oversight, deference to professional authority, and preference for favorable comparison.[2]

"Responsiveness" refers to the actions of state officials that correspond to the attitudes of their constituencies, which may or may not be articulated. Eulau and Quinley found that constituency opinion in this area usually had relatively low political salience, largely because little communication about higher education was received by legislators and other officials. When it was received, communication was sporadic, unorganized, and usually dealt with a specific issue rather than broad concerns.

State politicians perceived a general lack of interest among constituents but felt that the public was concerned about the admissions issue, that is, getting students into college. With regard to education issues, public schools far outweighed higher education in perceived salience. It should be added that other pressures on state officials—insufficient time and staff, the degree of interest in higher education, and the complexity of the issues—also promoted noninvolvement.

Legislative oversight of government agencies is part of the American tradition. In higher education, however, legislators generally seemed to feel that it should be largely limited to budgetary matters and broad policy guidelines. The rationale for this general posture was based, first, on traditions of academic freedom and keeping politics out of higher education and, second, on a feeling

---

[1] A similar analysis, based on the federal experience, appears in Samuel Halperin, "Politicians and Educators: Two World Views," *Phi Delta Kappan* 61 (November 1974): 189-90.

[2] The complete study is reported in Heinz Eulau and Harold Quinley, *State Officials and Higher Education* (New York: McGraw-Hill, 1970), and Heinz Eulau, "Political Norms Affecting Decisions Concerning Higher Education," in *Higher Education for Everybody?*, ed. W. Todd Furniss (Washington, D.C.: American Council on Education, 1971), pp. 207-23. This section draws, in part, from Julius C. C. Edelstein and Frederick S. Lane, "The Politics of Higher Education Is Also Politics" (Paper prepared for presentation at the Annual Conference of the New York State Political Science Association, March 1977, Albany, N.Y.).

that professional judgment was often required and that politicians were not really qualified in this regard. Given the relatively low political salience and the constraints already discussed, such as a busy schedule and a small staff, this posture was quite realistic. Eulau and Quinley found, as had earlier researchers, that when institutions were perceived to act irresponsibly and state officials felt forced to act, they would indeed take action, as they did against university administrators who were reluctant to control student unrest. However, they generally preferred quiescence.

Deference to professional authority was also an important political norm. Higher education issues are often complex and require detailed knowledge. Little knowledge and a lack of expertise led legislators and other state officials to depend on those who appeared to be knowledgeable, if often self-selected—university presidents, executive agencies and state higher education boards, and legislative committees and their chairpersons. While this conventional rule was often resented, the appearance of specialization—often highly institutionalized—appeared to be critical.

The final political norm that was important to state higher education policymaking in the 1960s was a preference for favorable comparison—that is, officials in one state would be able to compare their higher education structures and activities favorably with those in other states. Many states focused on the pacesetters, California and New York, which tended to watch one another. States in different areas often resorted to regional comparisons, such as "best in the South."

These four political norms affected the interface between state officials and higher education during the 1960s. In the last ten years, however, a great deal occurred that has affected state policymaking in higher education. State officials now apparently hold four somewhat different political norms regarding higher education—low responsiveness, activism in policy formulation and oversight, skepticism of professional authority, and preference for priority setting. Low responsiveness is the only norm that continues to prevail. By and large, higher education issues still have low political salience. The most salient single issue—providing sufficient room for those seeking college—has, if anything, been reversed. Declining enrollments frequently mean excess capacity. Now education officials are communicating with legislators, but only rarely in a way that is perceived as representative and politically intense. If any issue has emerged as salient, it is helping students—or their parents—to pay for college. State officials have largely rejected passivity in favor of an activist posture in formulating and overseeing policies. This activism is largely a function of the increased publicness of American higher education. The expansion in terms of enrollment occurred primarily in the 1960s with the growth in the number and size of public institutions of higher education. A great increase in the appropriations of public funds for both operating and capital expenditures accompanied the expansion of the role of the public sector in higher education. The existence of mass higher education, in terms of both students and public expenditures, along with student activism beginning in the late 1960s, increased the political visibility of higher education and produced calls for accountability.

Such activism is often led by the governor. As the Carnegie Commission on Higher Education commented, in its 1971 report, *The Capitol and the Campus:* "The potential influence of a governor over public higher education in his state is perhaps greater than any other single force affecting the state's public colleges and universities." The governor has three main roles in the governance of higher education—the state's chief executive, chief budget officer, and chief opinion leader. As chief executive, the governor often appoints members to the statewide coordinating board, as well as to the boards of trustees of individual public institutions. Also as chief executive, the governor signs or vetoes, encourages or discourages, or initiates new legislation affecting higher education, often private as well as public. The governor frequently reviews and approves or disapproves, formally or informally, statewide plans for postsecondary education.

As chief budget officer, the governor, assisted by a budget staff, recommends and approves annual budgetary appropriations for higher education. This role provides the governor with considerable influence over the operational decisions of the entire higher education structure. In a period of state-level budgetary reductions, budget decisions often become higher educational policy decisions of the most fundamental kind. The governor, who holds office through election by the voters of an entire state, also leads public opinion on matters relating to higher education. This role is particularly important in relations with other members of the same political party, higher education boards, the press, and a variety of citizen and educational groups.

An uneasy partnership exists between the state legislatures and higher education. Here the different perspectives of politicians and academics seem greatest, and tension inevitably follows. The legislature would be formidable if only because of its budgetary role, and the increased visibility of higher education together with the political economy of the states since the mid-1970s has further promoted legislative activism in higher education. Legislative modernization and staff professionalization in the last fifteen years have also served to make legislatures more formidable participants in policymaking. Performance audits of higher education, such as those in Illinois and Virginia, have further intensified the legislative role. Intervention by state officials in certain areas—admissions, tuition, new campus planning, race-related issues, and sometimes new program approval—has always been more likely. However, state officials now seek a much broader policy role.

Respect for and confidence in the academic profession have lessened significantly among parents, students, and citizens as well as state officials in the last ten years. The declining economic value of a college degree and unemployment of some college graduates are only two of the contributing factors. New skepticism toward professional authority has had an important impact on the relations between colleges and state government. Experiencing serious fiscal stringencies, state officials have also shown a preference for setting priorities and for weighing the benefits and costs of competing programs and interests. The preference for favorable comparison with other states has largely disappeared, and higher education has clearly lost whatever priority it had.

In this context, then, four trends seem especially important in higher education and government relations at the state level—the political fragmentation of the higher education community, the growth of statewide administrative coordinating agencies, the increased popularity of state-level review and termination of academic programs, and a new interest in state "reappropriation" of federally funded programs. The first trend is the result of increasing internal division and conflict among the groups that make up the higher education establishment in each state, including conflict between public and private institutions of higher education. Forty-one of the fifty states have authorized state financial assistance to "independent" colleges and universities, either through direct institutional support or aid to students attending private institutions. In aid for each full-time equivalent student, Alaska, Pennsylvania, Illinois, New York, and New Jersey have been the leaders. The competition for money and students continues between public and private colleges almost everywhere. In Ohio it was necessary to formulate a code of ethics that obligates colleges to provide accurate information about their curricula and services so they may "not detract from other institutions" of higher learning.

Competition for students and money between two- and four-year institutions is evident, especially in the public sector. Community colleges have attracted increasing numbers of students and solid community-based political support. A third division is among higher education's various estates—students and faculty as well as the institutions themselves. With the right of eighteen-year-olds to vote, the right to register in their university communities, and an increasing ability to articulate their political demands, students as well as their families are potentially the most significant of these estates. In addition, unionized faculty have often generated additional influence by using the labor movement's political muscle. For example, in the case of the unionization of the faculty of state colleges in Pennsylvania, the faculty choice of bargaining agent was greatly influenced by the perceived potential of the various contenders to represent faculty interest in state government.

In the 1960s, state officials increasingly favored centralized coordination in higher education and, with it, policy direction, long-range planning, and attempts to improve resource allocation. With the expansion of higher education and the need for centralized coordination, the trend toward statewide coordinating boards with increased authority grew. Only two states now have no such board of any kind. Statewide coordinating boards, called regents in some states, have had four primary functions—planning, often culminating in periodically issuing a statewide "master plan"; review and approval of academic programs; consolidation or recommendation to state officials of annual operating budgets; and approval of capital budgets or construction.

The main achievements of such boards have been generally in the area of planning: controlling the expansion of new campuses and academic programs, extending educational opportunity, and promoting differentiation among institutions. At the same time, several studies have revealed that such planning has often failed to eliminate unnecessary program duplication, has not promoted interinstitutional cooperation, generally avoided the issue of quality, and failed to integrate the development of private and public colleges.

New factors that tend to increase the authority and functions of these boards include the intensified competition of higher education with other state functions for increasingly scarce state funds, hence the need for statewide representation and a unified voice for higher education; the critical attention that state officials now pay to higher education, indicated by the scrutiny of executive and legislative auditors; the increased use by coordinating boards of computerized information systems and modern decisional technologies; pressure to coordinate state adaptation to projected enrollment decline; the growth in state expenditures directed to private or "independent" institutions of higher education; and the responsibility of these agencies in many states for coordinating all of postsecondary education rather than just the collegiate sector. Given the current nature of state-level budgetary politics, many observers believe that colleges and universities, both public and private, will ironically have to give up some of their individual authority in order for higher education as a whole to maintain its influence. The vehicle may be the growing authority of these statewide coordinating boards.

The third state-level trend is the evaluation, elimination, and consolidation of academic programs. The role of the coordinating board in approving new programs is largely established, but program review and elimination have met a great deal of opposition. This process largely originated in New York, where the Regents Commission on Doctoral Education in 1973 concluded that there were more than enough Ph.D. and Ed.D. programs to meet the state's foreseeable needs. They found that expansion of doctoral programs had taken place, for the most part, among the state's weaker institutions and that the proliferation of doctoral programs had lowered educational quality. The report recommended that the regents review all doctoral programs in the state with an eye toward eliminating marginal programs, saving the public money, and raising the overall quality of the doctoral degree. The regents accepted this recommendation, and the State Education Department established a mechanism for reviewing doctoral programs by individual disciplines or fields. The State University of New York challenged the regents on this issue quite early in the process, but the courts have upheld the regents' authority. Other states have been watching the New York example quite closely. At least half of the nation's higher education coordinating boards are undertaking such program reviews, and these are not necessarily limited to doctoral programs.

The growth of federal involvement in higher education is a second vitally important aspect of the changing politics of higher education, and it should be mentioned in the state context because of a recent development. If Congress ever approves the recommendation of the Advisory Commission on Intergovernmental Relations (ACIR), federal appropriations to the states may have to be "reappropriated" at the state level. Even in the absence of federal action, the ACIR in February 1977 proposed model state-level legislation that would prohibit the expenditure of federal aid by a state agency unless the funds are appropriated by the legislature. Many states have demonstrated an interest in this new technique in intergovernmental relations, increasing the potential for expanding state authority in higher education in another direction.

Higher Education and the Federal Government

Generally conceived of as a state function, higher education had been of little or no direct concern to the federal government until recently. The Morrill Act of 1862 and the Second Morrill Act of 1890 expressed the first real concern, which was not actually demonstrated until the period 1958 to 1963. The basic charter for national higher education policy is generally considered in connection with the Higher Education Act of 1965 and the Education Amendments of 1972. President Nixon's "Higher Education" message to Congress in March 1970 was the first one devoted entirely to this subject.

The growth of the federal role in higher education can be accounted for by the confluence of interests that promoted federal involvement. The federal government, as well as foundations, was interested in harnessing some of the nation's best talent, often found in universities, to solve certain societal problems. Many government program administrators had been academics, and leading scholars often assisted in allocating federal funds. Universities and their administrators were interested in building their organizations' size, financial condition, and reputation. Their faculties sought to control independent funds, increase their personal income, expand their own research domain and reputation, attract good graduate students, and enjoy increased amenities, such as secretarial services and travel. Therefore, federal money and influence grew during and after World War II, especially in the 1960s.

The relationships between universities and political institutions have altered the public importance of American higher education. The result is what Edgar Litt calls the "public vocational university," one that is supported by federal funds, directed by governmental decisions, and dedicated to the production of applied knowledge and trained manpower useful to national political and economic leaders.[3] The federal government has been a full partner in supporting colleges and universities for some time. It influences higher education in a number of ways—through its emphasis on categorical programs, the level and conditions of funding, legislation of general interest that also affects higher education, and its information gathering activities.

There are many examples of federal regulations that affect higher education,

---

[3] Here and elsewhere the influence of Norman Birnbaum and others may be seen. See Carl Kaysen, ed., *Content and Context: Essays on College Education* (New York: McGraw-Hill, 1973).

and university administrators have complained increasingly about them. These regulations include equal opportunity policies in connection with student admissions and faculty personnel processes, environmental impact considerations in connection with capital construction, student-consumer protection in the content of college catalogues and brochures, admission of American-born medical students transferring from universities outside the United States, privacy regulations in the maintenance of student records, occupational health and safety regulations, facilitating equal access to facilities by the handicapped, the retirement age of faculty, and limitations on photocopying.

The relationships can be much more direct and troubling than these. Harvard University and the Central Intelligence Agency (CIA) have disagreed about security operations and recruiting by faculty members. During the Watergate revelations, the academic community discovered that White House staff and perhaps even the president considered cutting federal research funds to the Massachusetts Institute of Technology because its head, a former presidential science adviser, was opposed to antiballistic missiles. Moreover, CIA and FBI covert activities in the late 1960s and early 1970s went far beyond even some of the contentions of student protesters.

Despite the increasing quantity of paperwork, the rising cost of compliance with federal regulations, and even a profound federal influence, there is no national direction or plan for higher education. According to one estimate, some 439 federal programs affect higher education, involving congressional consideration by eighteen separate committees in the House of Representatives, sixteen committees in the Senate, and the Joint Committee on Atomic Energy.

Such a fragmentation also occurs in the executive branch. The Office of Education, which is involved in a remarkably small fraction of these programs, certainly does not provide central direction, and the long-term implications of the creation of a Department of Education remain far from clear. The cleavages and conflicts within the higher education community at the state level also appear in the national arena. Independent institutions strive for a national policy for private higher education. Community colleges—a strong political force—pursue their own interests. Certain associations of colleges and universities are older, more prestigious, or simply abler than others.

Following ten years of efforts to improve access to higher education for low-income students, pressures are mounting for greater assistance to middle income students. While there is some evidence to the contrary, middle class families in this period of economic recession are under an increasing strain in meeting the costs of college attendance. These pressures again raise questions about the degree of egalitarianism in American higher education and American society in general.

Policy Implications

Two-thirds of the direct cost of higher education is now paid by the public. The principle of accountability at the state or federal level suggests that it is not too much to ask that such funds be expended prudently, efficiently, and effectively. Certain requirements are inherent in the categorical approach to funding public programs. It seems only fair, then, to ask institutions of higher education fully and honestly to disclose their spending practices, treat consumers fairly, and cooperate in important national public policies in the area of civil rights. At the same time, educators have to contend with constantly changing reporting requirements, a variety of reporting forms for different agencies, and conflicting regulations. Clearly, there is ample evidence that the trend toward increased politicization and regulation of higher education must be reversed.

Discussions of reversing existing patterns of government control of higher education often start with two myths. The first myth is that "self-regulation" is a viable alternative. In health care, law enforcement, and military operations, the argument for self-regulation is unacceptable. Why should it be acceptable for higher education? Who would accept it? At the same time, it must be admitted that more responsible behavior by universities can build greater respect for these institutions.

The second myth is that it is possible to obtain some sort of special regulatory treatment for higher education. While such institutions are unique and important, so are public schools, hospitals, and the environment. There is no question that the nature of colleges and universities and their operation should be better understood by government officials at all levels, but special status is unlikely.

Government involvement in higher education will continue. Indeed, government support is essential to the continued development of higher education in the last quarter of the twentieth century. But institutions of higher education and the important societal interests that they represent can alter their limited role in government policymaking in three specific ways.

First, the higher education community can help government officials understand the "benefits of disorder." As one studies higher education in other industrialized nations, the pluralism and diversity of American higher education, as well as its strengths, become clear. To have the governance of higher education dispersed among fifty states is an advantage. To have research universities and community colleges as well as public and private universities in such a "system" promotes quality, innovation, and responsiveness. Comparative analyses reveal that a healthy private higher education sector is fundamentally important to the integrity of all American higher education. This long-term understanding could substantially influence higher education policymaking in state capitals and in Washington. Second, the higher education community can articulate its own cause. It must propose alternative legislation, communicate clearly with politicians, and work to change regulations. No distasteful regulation should ever be accepted as permanent, and accountability need not always be distasteful. Even more fundamentally, higher education must minimize its own conflicts in order to change the attitudes of the public and politicians and to eliminate their stereotypes of academics. Finally, higher educational institutions need fully to understand and to document the financial costs of regulation, especially federal regulation, and to seek modification or reimbursement for them.

The expanding government role in higher education has shifted much higher educational policymaking authority to public officials. But the debate has only begun. A dynamic balance between autonomy and control in higher education has always been needed. Universities are already, perhaps inherently, political institutions, and they have tended to become even more political. Accordingly, autonomy will become an increasingly important and contested issue, especially in the light of any differences in values between the academy and the polity.

The Case of Israel

ELAD PELED

Israel's educational system, a highly centralized national one since its beginning, has moved only recently toward a more decentralized one. It is of mutual interest to Israel and America to examine the phenomenon of a highly centralized national system of education in order better to understand the implications of this kind of system, its costs, and its benefits. Some lessons may be learned from the Israeli experience, but generalizations based on it should be drawn very carefully, because of the differences between the two environments and systems.

Comparing the national, centralized and the local, decentralized concepts of educational governance in order to decide which is a "better" system requires an examination of the results of the two systems. A significant variance in the results may lead one to look for a relationship between educational outcomes and educational governance. Although this kind of research is beyond the scope of this essay, the implications of a highly centralized and nationalized system of education will be discussed.

However, the political and administrative structure of an educational system does not solely determine its educational effects. Furthermore, the structure and organization of educational systems are generally their responses to extraeducational constraints, demands, and pressures and not the result of educational needs. Therefore, one should look to the social and political environment in order to understand an educational system. Israel's political culture may help explain some of the characteristics of its educational system. The Israeli experience indicates that a centralized educational system, like a centralized political system, has inherent deficiencies—uniformity, conservatism, and bureaucratization—that frequently exceed the benefits of centralization. Israel is a new society, founded by a self-selected population that migrated to territories perceived to be essentially uninhabited at the time of their settlement. As in the United States, the settlers underwent a frontier experience and had to covenant or contract with one another to create social and political institutions.[1]

---

[1] Daniel J. Elazar, "The Compound Structure of Public Service Delivery Systems," *Urban Affairs Annual Review* 12 (1977).

Israel's present political culture is still emergent, and it contains a number of conflicting elements. Principal among these are a statist-bureaucratic political culture that implicitly accepts the concept of a reified state existing independently of its citizens and that views political organization as essentially centralized, hierarchical, and bureaucratic (a view shared by the vast majority of Israelis from continental Europe); an Oriental subject political culture, which views government as the private preserve of an elite, functioning to serve the interests of that elite, and hence a potentially malevolent force in the lives of ordinary people (a view shared by the great majority of Israelis from the subject cultures of Eastern Europe and the Arab countries of the Middle East and North Africa); and a Jewish political culture, which is civic and republican in its orientation, viewing the polity as a partnership of fundamentally equal citizens entitled to an equal share of the benefits resulting from the pooling of common resources. This third culture combines a high level of citizen participation with a clear responsibility on the part of the governing authorities to set the polity's overall direction. This culture is shared to a lesser or greater degree by the 85 percent of the population that is Jewish.[2]

Daniel J. Elazar sees an uneasy tension between these three political cultures, which is evident in a great gap between the formal institutional structure of the polity—an expression of a European statism—and the actual political behavior and informal institutional arrangements that make it work. Formally, Israel is a highly centralized, hierarchically structured, bureaucratic state, but in fact its political system functions on the basis of myriad contractual agreements that assume widespread power-sharing on a decentralized basis. These agreements are enforced through a process of mutual consultation and negotiation in which all parties to an agreement must be conciliated before action is taken.

Characteristics of Israel's Educational System

Israel's educational system is bilingual; 85 percent of its pupils attend Hebrew-speaking schools, and 15 percent attend Arabic-speaking schools. Almost 50 percent of the Jewish pupils in the school system are disadvantaged children. The majority of these are Oriental Jews who come from North Africa or Arab countries in the Middle East. The state is exclusively responsible for educating its children. As stated by the minister who submitted the appropriate legislation in 1953, "Education is a state's domain, within its responsibilities and under its authority. . . . The state is ultimately responsible for the ways through which the development of the young generation will be directed and realised."[3] This postulate is illustrated by a centralized system directed, financed, and controlled by the Ministry of Education and Culture.

Ideological orientation has been a predominant factor in Israel's educational system since the prestate era, before 1948. Hence, the schools have a social and

---

[2] Ibid.

[3] Ben-Zion Dinur, "The State Law of Education," in *Values and Ways*, ed. Ben-Zion Dinur (Tel Aviv: Urim, 1958).

national mission, rather than an orientation directed toward the welfare of the individual. Education is virtually free but not compulsory for children between ages three and four, free and compulsory between the ages of five and sixteen, and free but not compulsory between ages seventeen and eighteen. The law grants parents the right to choose between a state, religious education and a state, nonreligious education. Israel's educational system has been characterized since its inception by inherent conflicts, such as egalitarianism versus elitism; uniformity versus diversity; centralization versus decentralization; competitiveness and achievement orientation versus noncompetitiveness and social orientation; ideological orientation versus nonideological orientation; predominance of national and social objectives versus child-centered orientation; continuity and traditionalism versus innovation; predominance of a traditional orthodox Jewish orientation versus a mix of Jewish and general, modern orientation; recognition of the uniqueness and special needs of an Arab education versus a uniform approach toward the Arab curriculum.

These tensions are consequences of Israel's present social situation and stem both from external constraints and from the historical development of the Jewish educational system in Israel before 1948. The Israeli educational system, its psychological and pedagogical concepts, and the perceptions and attitudes developed in this system must be viewed in the context of these characteristics. The nationalized and centralized nature of Israel's education is reflected in many aspects of the system. This essay discusses only a few, very important ones: goals and objectives, curriculum, the feedback process, the role of the educational bureaucracy, the policymaking process, and school finance.

Israel's educational policymakers have always been society-oriented. They regard educational objectives as based on a philosophy of life, on the specific characteristics of the society and its necessities, and on the needs of the pupil. The definition of these characteristics and needs depends, at least partially, on the social norms, values, and biases.

The vital need for national unity on one hand and political conflicts and tensions on the other led the "founding fathers" of Israel to the compromise found in the somewhat vaguely stated educational objectives of section 2 of the State Education Law of 1953: "The object of 'State Education' is to base elementary education in the state on the values of Jewish culture and the achievements of science, on the love of the homeland and the loyalty to the state and the Jewish people, on practice of agricultural work and handicraft, on pioneer (haluzic) training and on striving for a society built on freedom, equality, tolerance, mutual assistance and love of mankind." It should be noted that democratic societies that legislate their educational objectives view them as a political act representing a general consensus or a statement of the will of the majority. As such, the legislation of educational objectives helps to mobilize support and has an integrative and cohesive impact on the society. This was one of the goals of the Israeli legislation regarding educational objectives, but its attainment may be questioned.

This nonoperational statement of objectives has been criticized by people who believe such a political compromise may lead to the alienation of the young generation from the traditions and inheritance of its ancestors.[4] Furthermore, some people claim that a democratic society should not formalize its educational objectives. Any legalization of this kind, they believe, must be viewed as an intervention in private domains, akin to intervention in the domains of beliefs and opinions. A draft of a master plan for education in Israel in the 1980s stated explicitly that Israel's special circumstances of survival and existence, both physically and ideologically, impose a necessity for having national objectives of education, despite contravening democratic norms.[5]

The basic philosophy of the nationalized system of education was stated clearly by the minister of education and culture, who presented the legislation of the state education to Israel's parliament (the Knesset) in 1953:

> State education means that education is an area under the State's jurisdiction, within its domain of activity and its full authority. . . . Education as a systematic and organized activity is a social action, directed by the public and within the boundaries of the organized society, and primarily within the State's responsibility. . . .
>
> Political independence means also that the responsibility for the preservation of the spiritual inheritance of the Nation is in the hands of the State, which is the organized unity of the Nation. Therefore, the State cannot give up—and nowhere does it—its full responsibility of the basic objectives and goals of any education. . . . It is the State's duty and obligation to educate its citizens to a complete identification of each individual with the State, with its future, with its survival.[6]

Consequently, in 1954–55 the Ministry of Education and Culture published new curricula, based on the State Law of Education of 1953, which abolished the three autonomous political organizations of education that existed before the declaration, and established a nonreligious school system and a religious school system under a unified state administration.

The new curricula were intended to implement the objectives of "State Education" by imposing uniform and mandatory curricula throughout the system, with recognized variations between religious and nonreligious schools. As these new curricula were being implemented, they were strongly criticized. The criticisms were directed at their uniformity and ideological basis rather than differentiation and a psychopedagogical base. Two additional arguments correctly foresaw that formulas of political compromises are noneducative and even cause alienation between children and their parents' generation and that mandatory, uniform curricula would encourage the excessive bureaucratization of the system. This is what has happened.

The dynamics of Israel's educational system and the influence of the New Curriculum movement in the United States in the late 1950s and the 1960s led to

---

[4] Zvi Lam, "İdeological Tensions: Conflicts About the Objectives," in *Education in Israel*, ed. Chaim Ormian (Jerusalem: Ministry of Education and Culture, 1973).

[5] Elad Peled, ed., *Education in Israel in the 1980's* (Jerusalem: Ministry of Education and Culture, 1976).

[6] Dinur.

curriculum innovation. The ministry sent a group of Israeli educators to the University of Chicago to be trained by B. S. Bloom and his colleagues. A parliamentary decision in 1968 about structural reform of the educational system gave momentum to the New Curriculum in the state system. The New Curriculum was intended to respond to the needs of the society and the individual pupil, as well as to the structure of the disciplines, the common educational philosophy, and recent findings of educational psychology. Once more, though innovative in spirit and form, the curriculum was uniform, with limited choice. The continuing dispute between educators who are entirely society-oriented and those who are entirely child-oriented and facing the challenge of low achievement by disadvantaged children, however, has resulted in a movement in recent years toward more differentiation and variation. Nonetheless, the conflict between uniformity and the autonomy of schools and teachers is still characteristic of the system.

Uniformity of curriculum was achieved not only by administrative regulations but even more by the leverage of standardized examinations and tests. The most important of these examinations is the Final Certificate, the Matriculation *(Bagrut)* of the academic high school. Originally this certificate was designed to select future students for higher education and was the culmination of learning in the school system. *Bagrut* is awarded on the basis of standardized, state-administered examinations and partially on teachers' assessments. Lower certificates (School Leaving Certificates after twelve years of studies) are not accepted by higher educational institutions.

As a consequence of these examinations, the curriculum became heavily geared to the final examinations, hence uniform. Teachers adhere closely to examination requirements, and instead of provoking feedback, the examination has become the primary goal for most teachers and students.

Bureaucratization of the System

The uniformity of the curriculum and the centralization of the administration contributed to bureaucratization. Legally, three persons control and administer the system: the minister of education and culture, a member of the cabinet, and a political figure, representing one of the political parties participating in the government coalition; the director-general of the ministry, the top professional civil-servant and the chief administrator of the system, appointed by the cabinet; and the director of the Religious Education Department in the ministry, appointed by the minister and holding important statutory responsibilities.

The system is distinctly divided between compulsory education (ages five to sixteen, grades K-10) and noncompulsory education (ages three to four, seventeen to eighteen, grades below K and 11-12). Generally, the ministry has direct responsibility for kindergarten and elementary schools and partial responsibility for junior high schools, while local municipalities or private or public organizations directly control and are responsible for kindergartens for three- to four-year olds and secondary schools. The basic difference between the two subsystems concerns the authority for hiring and firing teachers and school principals. For both subsystems the ministry has the dominant influence and control through the budget, curriculum, and achievement standards (standardized examinations), and the licensing of teachers.

Local authorities implement the ministry's policies and have direct responsibility for building and maintaining kindergarten, elementary, and secondary schools. Obviously, the autonomy of the school principal and the teachers is very narrow and frequently nonexistent. Furthermore, the supervisory system irritates teachers and creates a hierarchical and authoritative system of education, resulting in a conservative approach toward change and innovation, minimal teacher initiative, minimal capacity for responsiveness by a particular school or school district to the specific social or political needs and demands of its community and environment, a gap in communication and involvement between parents and educators that can alienate the two groups from each other, and conflict between the educational bureaucracy and the research establishment at the universities.

A central figure in the educational bureaucracy is the school supervisor, who is responsible for assigning and evaluating teachers, supervising the training and performance of teachers and principals, maintaining administrative authority over the principal, and supervising the implementation of the ministry's regulations. These functions give the supervisor a powerful position and make the supervisors an important interest group within the educational establishment.

Figure 1 illustrates the subjects of decisions and the foci of policymaking, distinguishing between the political (government) level and the administrative

FIGURE 1

The Policymaking Process in Israel's Educational System

	The Political Level			The Administrative Level				
	Ministry	Local Govern- ments	Parents	K-3-4	K-5	Elemen- tary School	Junior High School	Secon- dary School
Curriculum	X		25% of the syllabus (rarely exercised)					
Methods of teaching	X			X	X	X	X	X
Pupils, zoning, and registration		X						X
Teachers' appoint- ments and assign- ment	X*	X						X
Teachers' salary	X							
School construction	Budget allocations	X						
Building maintenance		X						

*Only for elementary schools and kindergarten to 5-year-old children.

(school) level. Based on this schema one may conclude that budgetary allocations are made almost exclusively within the ministry, while their utilization is
determined directly by the ministry—specifically, the salaries of kindergarten
and elementary school teachers—and partially by local municipalities or other
local school governments. The ministry assigns and appoints K-5 and elementary
school teachers, while local governments assign and appoint K-3-4 and secondary school teachers. The curriculum is almost exclusively the responsibility of
the ministry, while teaching methods are subject to the autonomy of local
schools and school teachers. The teacher salary scales are exclusively the
ministry's responsibility as are other budgetary standards, including maintenance and other adjunct services. Implementation of the ministry's policies is
based on several legal, formal, and informal instruments, including legislation
and administrative regulations, budgetary allocations, the final certification
examinations and standardized tests, the mandatory curriculum, and personnel
supervision.

School Finance

As in many other countries, politicians and educators in Israel still believe in a
direct link between money and better education and feel that the quality of
education, measured by learning achievements, results from the allocation of
"sufficient" resources to education. Therefore, the quality of education should
not depend on people's income and on their financial capability to support an
educational system. This "equality of educational opportunity" interpretation
as phrased by the California Supreme Court in *Serrano* v. *Priest* (1971) has been
practiced in Israel since the beginning of its school system.

School finance in Israel is based on two premises. First, the quantity of resources allocated to education results from a compromise between the needs
of education and the country's economic ability to satisfy them, as expressed
in the state budget. Second, there is no direct link between taxation and the
level of services that the citizen receives. Thus in Israel there is no inequality
in educational services that may be related to inequalities in the wealth and
income of taxpayers, though some inequalities in educational services do exist
as the result of other factors, such as manpower and citizens' motivation to be
involved in public activity.

The national government currently allocates 70 percent of its total expenditures to education, including higher education; local governments, 13 percent;
and citizens and nonprofit organizations, 17 percent. Individual payment for
educational services involves only kindergarten for ages three and four (a
graduated progressive tuition fee) and higher education. The rest of education
(ages five to sixteen) is free and largely compulsory.

Evaluation of the System

It is wrong to judge the system as good or bad without referring to specific
contexts and to priorities explicitly or implicitly defined as the main social and

political issues in question at the time. A centralized system enables national policymakers to impose their policies on the entire system relatively fast by exercising a number of powers, such as allocation of resources and administrative and legal powers. When there is an emergency or when national goals have a high priority, a centralized system is much more effective than a decentralized one. On the other hand, a decentralized system is better if individual rights, people's involvement and participation, and community control are preferred.

A centralized system of education is generally characterized as uniform, bureaucratic, and nonresponsive. Uniformity is illustrated in its content, curriculum, teaching methods, and learning standards; bureaucratization in its organization and political framework; and nonresponsiveness in the interaction between the system and local needs and demands.

A decentralized system, on the other hand, is generally characterized as diversified, autonomous, and responsive. Diversity is evident in content, curriculum, teaching methods, and learning standards; autonomy, in policymaking powers; and responsiveness, in regard to local needs.

Centralization of Israel's educational system was not planned or selected deliberately by its founders, but rather emerged as a combination of historical development, Zionist ideology, and social and political "environmental" processes accompanied by some sporadic planning. It should be noted that despite the strong impact of centralization in Israel's educational system, trends of decentralization could always be discerned. The most distinct example is the ideological, political, and educational controversy between orthodox and nonreligious Jews and the establishment of two separate school systems. Another illustration of decentralization is the effort of the kibbutz movement to protect and even expand its educational autonomy. These cases emphasize the political and ideological orientation and biases of Israel's politics. Elements of decentralization were introduced and legitimized in recognition of differences in ideology, but there is no similar recognition of individual or local rights in regard to education. Although there is no constitutional or historical tradition of "local rights" in Israel, local communities and local centers of power inevitably conflict with the central government, more through a long and tortuous process of eroding national policies during their implementation than through a direct confrontation.

Centralization of the educational system emerged first in the preindependence era as a political tool against the British colonial government and as a means of preserving Jewish autonomy. The emerging state of Israel faced two crucial challenges in its first decade and even later: military security and the absorption of massive immigration immediately after independence. The population more than doubled, from 650,000 in 1948 to 1,650,000 in 1952. Israel's education was called on to play a major role in meeting these challenges. Only a powerful centralized system could have met the challenge of educating the masses of immigrant children, most of them from Moslem countries. The main benefit of the centralization of Israel's educational system was the tremendous quantitative growth of the schools and their absorption of many immigrant children. The schools served as a major instrument in the melting pot policy.

One way of evaluating the organization of an educational system is by examining the process of policymaking through a specific case. The case chosen here is the process of introducing both educational and social innovations into the educational system.

The logic of Israel's highly centralized system may be described according to national goals, objectives, curriculum, and reforms. Education stems from the national goals of security, economic growth, absorbing immigrants, unifying the nation, and developing a Hebrew culture to continue the traditional Jewish culture adapted to the new environment of an independent state. The objectives of education derived from these national goals enacted in section 2 of the State Education Law of 1953. In order to implement national goals and the specifically defined objectives of education, a uniform curriculum was planned and imposed, and the organizational structure of the school system (eight years of elementary education and four years of secondary education) was expected to absorb the rapidly growing number of pupils. Two simultaneous developments acted both on and within the system: social pressures to narrow the social, political, and cultural gap between "Oriental" and "Western" Jews and the shocking phenomenon of low academic achievements of Oriental children. These environmental stresses forced the system to change and to innovate its structure, curriculum, and teaching methods.

Instead of a gradual process of change and innovation resulting from continuous feedback from schools and society to the policymaking process, the need for change required a dramatic reform, possible only through a policy imposed on the system from above. In the late 1960s, such a reform began by simultaneously preparing a new curriculum and modifying the traditional structure of eight years of elementary and four years of secondary education to a new structure of six years each, including three years of junior and of senior high school.

National goals again dominated, and educational policy interpreted them into educational objectives and strategies. In imposing the reforms, policymakers collided immediately with the educational bureaucracy. A long process of conflict developed, ending in a weak, eroded reform and embittered and alienated educational leaders.

Two methods were employed in Israel's educational system to ensure the implementation of its national goals: the establishment of national standards and examinations and of a hierarchical system of supervisors. Both retained the system's uniformity, reinforced its bureaucratic character, and strengthened its nonresponsiveness to local needs and demands. The process of spasmodic, superimposed reforms in a centralized system meant inevitable conflicts with the hierarchy of the existing educational bureaucracy. When change was required and a reform enacted and imposed, the old supervisors felt threatened and resisted the imposed reform. On the other hand, the most effective way to introduce the new curriculum was to co-opt the supervisors. The continuous pressure of imposed standards and curriculum through national examinations and supervision minimized the initiative of teachers and principals, encouraged compliance among teachers, and eliminated the initiative and creativity among teachers.

The Case of the Disadvantaged

In Israel, the top priority is given to narrowing the social and cultural gap between social groups through compensatory policy and school integration. Local interests have sometimes conflicted with this national goal when school integration was the issue.

Because a highly centralized system is sensitive and responsive to national interests, national goals, and national ideologies and values, it is less responsive to local needs and requirements. Those characteristics of the Israeli system illustrated by the curriculum and supervision issues may be further clarified by the national policy of school integration or desegregation that frequently conflicted with the local interests of homogeneous neighborhood schools.

The challenge of advancing disadvantaged children has become the major issue in Israeli education and the first priority of its policy since the mid-1960s. Forty-seven percent of the elementary school pupils in 1975 were classified as disadvantaged. Ninety-five percent of this group were Orientals from large families with fathers whose education ended after elementary school. The policy of fostering the disadvantaged was based on the concepts of gap and variety. The gap represents the difference between the potential achievement of an individual or a group under optimal conditions and their actual achievements, while variety indicates differences in character, individual skills, tradition, customs, and cultural patterns and behaviors among groups.

Educational policy in Israel has aimed to narrow gaps as well as to encourage variety. The strategies of coping with the issue of the disadvantaged in Israel developed through different approaches and stages. Since the middle 1950s the different strategies included compensatory education, organizational reform, and massive financial aid together with more local involvement and participation, and school integration. Studies published in 1976 revealed that these policies had not significantly changed the gap between the average academic achievements of Oriental and Western children. At the same time, progress in basic skills in lower grades, an increase in school attendance in the elementary and secondary schools, and an important expansion of vocational education were reported. These changes may in time lead to changes in the gaps. Meanwhile, Israel's educational policymakers are still looking for better ways to respond to the continuous challenge of closing the gap. The point is that despite the power and options of Israel's highly centralized system, it appeared unable to solve a crucial educational issue, and one may doubt its ability to solve other major problems.

In conclusion, nobody can say definitely whether a centralized or decentralized system is better. The normative answer depends on other factors. If its biggest challenge is the absorption of immigrants and the development of national unity, then the best solution is a centralized system. If, on the other hand, the approach is pluralistic, and if local democracy, citizen involvement and participation, and the need for educational innovations are the major issues, then the centralized system may be counterproductive. Nevertheless, this brief examination of Israel's educational system does not indicate that a centralized system can always solve its crucial educational problems.

Index